RAJNAARA C. AKHTAR,
PATRICK NASH AND
REBECCA PROBERT

COHABITATION AND RELIGIOUS MARRIAGE

Status, Similarities and Solutions

BRISTOL
UNIVERSITY
PRESS

First published in Great Britain in 2020 by

Bristol University Press
1-9 Old Park Hill
Bristol
BS2 8BB
UK
t: +44 (0)117 954 5940
www.bristoluniversitypress.co.uk

British Library Cataloguing in Publication Data
A catalogue record for this book is available from the British Library

ISBN 978-1-5292-1083-5 hardcover
ISBN 978-1-5292-1085-9 ePub
ISBN 978-1-5292-1084-2 ePdf

Cover design by Blu Inc
Front cover image: iStock / Vershinin
Printed and bound in the UK by CPI Group (UK) Ltd, Croydon, CR0 4YY
Bristol University Press uses environmentally responsible print partners

MIX
Paper from responsible sources
FSC® C013604

Contents

Table of Cases

A-M v A-M (Divorce: jurisdiction: validity of marriage) [2001] 2 FLR 6

AAA v ASH [2009] EWHC 636 (Fam)

AI v MT [2013] EWHC 100

Akhter v Khan [2018] EWFC 54, *Attorney General v Akhter and Khan* [2020] EWCA Civ 122

Asaad v Kurter [2013] EWHC 3852 (Fam)

Azad v Entry Clearance Officer Dhaka [2001] INLR 109

Bibi v Chief Adjudication Officer [1998] 1 FLR 375

Chief Adjudication Officer v Bath [2000] 1 FLR 8

Choudhury v Choudhury [2006] EWHC 1837 (Ch)

Collett v Collett [1968] P 482

Crake v Supplementary Benefits Commission [1982] 1 All ER 498

Dukali v Lamrani [2012] EWHC 1748 (Fam)

ECO New Delhi v SG [2012] UKUT 00265 (IAC)

El Gamal v Al Maktoum [2011] EWHC B27 (Fam)

Gereis v Yagoub [1997] 1 FLR 854

Ghandi v Patel [2001] EWHC Ch 473

Gow v Grant [2012] UKSC 29

Hudson v Leigh [2009] EWHC 1306 (Fam)

Hyman v Hyman [1929] AC 601

Imam Din v National Assistance Board [1967] 2 QB 213

Jones v Kernott [2011] UKSC 53

Kohn v Wagschal & Ors [2007] EWCA Civ 1022

Kotke v Saffarini [2005] EWCA Civ 221

Langford v Secretary of State for Defence [2019] EWCA Civ 1271

Lloyds Bank v Rosset [1991] 1 AC 107

MA v JA and the Attorney General [2012] EWHC 2219 (Fam)

McLaughlin, Re Judicial Review (Northern Ireland) [2018] UKSC 48

Miller v Miller; McFarlane v McFarlane [2006] UKHL 24

MS (Somalia) v Secretary of State for the Home Department), [2010] Imm AR 242

Nabi (Ghulam) v Heaton (Inspector of Taxes) [1981] 1 WLR 1052

RB v UK (Bibi v UK) App No 19628/92, ECmHR decision of 29 June 1992

R (Elmes) v Essex CC) [2019] 1 WLR 1686

R (ota Steinfeld and Keidan) v Secretary of State for International Development (in substitution for the Home Secretary and the Education Secretary) [2018] UKSC 32

R v Bham [1965) 3 All ER 124

R v Immigration Appeal Tribunal Ex. p. Begum (Hasna) [1995] Imm AR 249

R v Kemp; R v Else [1964] 2 QB 344

Radmacher v Granatino [2010] UKSC 42

Re Brewster for Judicial Review (Northern Ireland) [2017] UKSC 8

Re Smyth's Application for Judicial Review [2017] NIQB 55; [2018] NICA 25

Re Spence, dec'd [1990] Ch 652

S v S [2014] EWHC 7 (Fam)

Sharbatly v Shagroon [2012] EWCA Civ 1507

Stack v Dowden [2007] UKHL 17

T and M v OCC and C [2010] EWHC 964

V v V (Prenuptial Agreement) [2012] 1 FLR 1315

Table of Legislation

Statutes

Adoption and Children Act 2002
Antisocial Behaviour, Crime and Policing Act 2014
Arbitration Act 1996
Child Support Act 1991
Children Act 1989
Civil Partnerships, Marriages and Deaths (Registration etc) Act 2019
Civil Registration (Amendment) Act 2012
Civil Registration Act 2004
Clandestine Marriages Act 1753
Criminal Law Act 1977
Family Law (Scotland) Act 2006
Family Law Act 1996
Family Law Reform Act 1987
Human Fertilisation and Embryology Act 2008
Inheritance (Provision for Family and Dependants) Act 1975
Legal Aid, Sentencing and Punishment of Offenders Act 2012
Legitimacy Act 1976
Marriage (Northern Ireland) Order 2003
Marriage (Same Sex Couples) Act 2013
Marriage (Scotland) Act 1977
Marriage Act 1823
Marriage Act 1836
Marriage Act 1898
Marriage Act 1949
Marriage Act 1994
Marriage and Civil Partnership (Scotland) Act 2014
Matrimonial and Family Proceedings Act 1984
Matrimonial Causes Act 1973

Northern Ireland (Executive Formation etc) Act 2019
Police and Criminal Evidence Act 1984
Private International Law (Miscellaneous Provisions) Act 1995
Rent Act 1977
Serious Crime Act 2005
Sexual Offences Act 2003
Social Security Contributions and Benefits Act 1992
Trustees of Land and Appointment of Trustees Act 1996

Bills

Arbitration and Mediation Services (Equality) Bill [HL] 2016–17
Cohabitation Rights Bill [HL] 2008–09
Cohabitation Rights Bill [HL] 2017–19

Notes on Contributors

Rajnaara C. Akhtar is Senior Lecturer at Leicester De Montfort University Law School and Visiting Scholar in Residence at Georgetown University in Qatar. Her research interests focus on marriage formalities and unregistered religious-only marriages. Her research into informal marriages looks at transitional relationship norms, legal consequences and law reform. She has conducted extensive empirical fieldwork on this area in the UK, Qatar and Australia. She received her PhD from the University of Warwick in 2013.

Amin Al-Astewani is Lecturer at Lancaster Law School. His research focuses on the role played by religious tribunals in western legal systems and he has conducted empirical research in this area. He submitted written evidence to Parliament as part of the government's first public review of Sharia Councils in the UK. As part of his engagement with community organizations and bodies, he has also advised the UK Board of Sharia Councils on the legal status of religious tribunals. He continues to offer his expertise and advice to both policy makers and Sharia Councils on the legal status and role of Islamic tribunals in the English legal system.

Anne Barlow is Professor of Family Law and Policy at the University of Exeter Law School, which she joined in 2004 from the University of Wales, Aberystwyth, having previously practised as a solicitor in London. She is a Law with French graduate of Sussex University and has also studied at the College of Law, London and the University of Strasbourg. She has a particular interest in family law and policy, especially the regulation of adult relationships such as cohabitation and marriage, but has also taught and researched in the areas of comparative law, housing law and welfare law and policy.

Joanna Miles is Reader in Family Law and Policy at the University of Cambridge. She has been a Fellow of Trinity College since 1999 and was appointed University Lecturer in 2007 following a two-year secondment as a team lawyer to the Law Commission for England and Wales working on its Cohabitation project between 2005 and 2007. She was appointed Senior Lecturer in October 2011 and then Reader from October 2017.

Zainab Naqvi completed her LLB (Law and French) at Coventry University in 2012 and was awarded her Masters degree from the University of Birmingham Law School in 2013. She continued at Birmingham as an ESRC DTC Doctoral Researcher. She was appointed Lecturer in Law at Coventry University in 2017 and then moved to Leicester De Montfort University Law School as Senior Lecturer in January 2020. Her research interests are in family law and socio-legal theory, with a particular focus on legal responses to relationships and marriages in the UK.

Patrick Nash (LLB, MSc, PhD, FHEA, BPTC) completed his ESRC-funded doctoral thesis in 2016 at the University of Bristol on the question 'How Should English Law Relate to Islam?' He taught jurisprudence, public law, criminal law, tort law and family law at Bristol Law School and Newcastle Law School before joining the Woolf Institute in Cambridge as a Research Fellow in October 2018. He concurrently took up a BPTC scholarship and was called to the Bar of England and Wales in 2019 (Lincoln's Inn). He was admitted to St Edmund's College at the University of Cambridge as a Post-Doctoral Research Associate in October 2019.

Rehana Parveen received her PhD from the University of Birmingham and is currently a Lecturer there. Her research focuses on the area of Islamic/Sharia law and its positioning in English law, particularly with regard to matrimonial and family disputes which are resolved through Sharia-based tribunals or Sharia Councils. She is a former solicitor and former senior tutor at The University of Law, teaching on the GDL, LPC and BPTC courses.

Rebecca Probert is Professor of Law at Exeter University Law School, which she joined in April 2017. She has a particular interest in family law and legal history. She has written on all aspects of modern family law although her main research interests lie in the overlapping areas of marriage, cohabitation, bigamy and divorce.

Islam Uddin completed his PhD at Middlesex University on the topic of 'Muslim Family Law: British-Bangladeshi Muslim Women and Divorce in the UK'. He also received a Masters degree in Islamic Studies from Middlesex University. He is an Imam and a lecturer, teaching classical and contemporary Islamic law. He regularly delivers sermons and lectures to mosques, colleges, universities and other community organizations throughout the UK.

Vishal Vora (PhD) is a Research Fellow at the Department of Law and Anthropology, Max Planck Institute for Social Anthropology in Halle (Saale), Germany. His current research focuses on the maturing British Hindu community, examining the relationship between religion and state, in particular the community search for its identity in multicultural Britain.

Acknowledgements

This volume is the culmination of a range of research findings presented and discussed during a one-day symposium held at the Institute of Advanced Legal Studies in London in December 2018. The symposium was co-convened by Rajnaara Akhtar (De Montfort University), Patrick Nash (Woolf Institute, Cambridge), Rebecca Probert (University of Exeter) and Russell Sandberg (University of Cardiff), under the umbrella of INSRUM (International Network of Scholars Researching Unregistered Marriages). Titled *Relationship Breakdown; Informal and Legal Solutions*, the event gathered a number of voices, including academics, campaigners, legal practitioners and the judiciary. We are grateful to all of the authors who submitted papers and the many others who presented papers or participated at the symposium, including Professor Gillian Douglas for the keynote address, Frank Cranmer, Sharon Thompson, Kathryn O'Sullivan, Susan Leahy, Felicity Belton, Anne-Marie Hutchinson QC and Mr Justice Williams. Our thanks are also extended to Bristol University Press, in particular Rebecca Tomlinson, Helen Davis and Freya Trand. We are also grateful to the Law School at De Montfort University for their generous funding of the event.

Finally, we would like to acknowledge our special gratitude to the late Valentine Le Grice QC for his support and contribution to the final panel discussion. Val's passing merely days after the symposium was a terrible loss for us all, and for the whole of the family law community in the UK and beyond.

ONE

Introduction

Rajnaara C. Akhtar, Patrick Nash and Rebecca Probert[1]

In recent years, there has been a rise in both the number of cohabiting couples and those entering into religious-only marriages in England and Wales. Cohabitants are the fastest-growing relationship type, numbering 3.4 million (ONS, 2019), while up to 60 per cent of Muslim couples marrying are thought to be in religious-only marriages (True Vision, 2017). Although these relationship types are conceptually different, with the parties having divergent motivations and beliefs, in both cases the result is all too often inadequate legal protection when the relationship ends, with those who have gone through a religious-only marriage generally having no more rights than those who have gone through no ceremony at all. Despite this shared legal framework, the linkages and overlaps between these two groups have largely been ignored in research, literature and government policy responses. This volume is the first to bring together scholars working in both areas to explore the complexities of the law, the different ways in which individuals experience and navigate the legal framework, and the potential paths for law reform.

---

1 At the time of writing, Rebecca Probert is providing expert advice to the Law Commission on their review of weddings law. Nothing in this work should be taken as representing the views of the Law Commission.

This range of intersecting issues is explored by authors at the forefront of current research, providing a unique overview of this complex and controversial area. Each author proposes evidence-based law reform, responding to the need for research-led policy recommendations in this area. The issue of Muslim religious-only marriages, in particular, has drawn responses from campaigners seeking to protect women from poor outcomes on relationship breakdown. These legitimate efforts to influence policy need to be seen in the context of the more wide-ranging evidence gathered from a broad spectrum of participants, as well as the equally poor outcomes suffered by women in cohabiting relationships.

We begin by examining wedding law, outlining when a marriage should be considered valid, void or not recognized at all (Probert, Chapter Two). The volume then goes on to look at the legal treatment of couples in informal relationships, whether a religious-only marriage, a relationship preceded by some non-formal ceremony, or cohabitation without any ceremony (Miles, Chapter Three), and the assumptions held by cohabitants and those in religious-only marriages in the light of their 'lived experiences' (Barlow, Chapter Four).

Following this scene setting, we move on to consider the adequacy of the current law, beginning by appraising the 'non-marriage/non-qualifying ceremony' category, often (though not exclusively) linked to Muslim religious-only marriages (Vora, Chapter Five). The problematization of Muslim religious-only marriages is tackled, with a solution which covers all families within cohabiting relationships being advocated (Akhtar, Chapter Six). Another proposal for law reform is for a post-ceremony registration to encourage more couples to engage with simplified legal formalities, similar to the registration of a birth or death (Parveen, Chapter Seven). Taking a holistic view of women's autonomy in choice of relationship form, the issue of polygyny is raised to broaden religious-only marriage narratives, arguing for recognition of religious marriages, with an option for the couple to mutually agree to opt out of legal recognition (Naqvi, Chapter Eight).

We then proceed to focus on dispute resolution, critically appraising the role of Sharia Councils in granting religious divorces, and advocating a 'Standard of Practice' to be voluntarily adhered to by these bodies (Uddin, Chapter Nine). The role of arbitration is then explored, utilizing the Muslim Arbitration Tribunal as a case study to advocate for a model which conforms to the Family Arbitration Scheme to enable family arbitration in disputes involving religious marriages (Al-Astewani, Chapter Ten). Finally, the case for moving towards a minimalistic law of marriage is presented, in light of the shortcomings and complexity of the current wedding laws and the need for religious-only marriages to refer disputes to non-state forums (Nash, Chapter Eleven).

The themes, concepts and ideas presented and developed here include the manifestation and forms of cohabitation, the relationship between the state and religion, and what role, if any, religious tribunals should have in dealing with the consequences of relationship breakdown; gender inequality and agency in family law and family practice; cultural norms and transitions, including the evolving nature of the 'family'; and the retreat of the state from the regulation of families. These themes are relevant both to cohabiting couples and those in religious-only marriages. This introductory chapter sets the scene, focusing on 'status, similarities and solutions'.

Cohabitation and religious marriage: status

The law in this area is in much need of reform. It has evolved at a slow pace, often left trailing behind in the wake of new and evolving relationship norms. In modern societies, the need for laws that respond to lived realities has never been more pertinent. Whether it is a question of where to marry, how to marry or the form of commitment a couple makes to each other, it is clear that increasing numbers of families are being left without family law protections on relationship breakdown. As a result, there has been a growing demand for reform of the law relating to the rights of cohabiting couples and the legal formalities required for state-recognized marriages.

Cohabitants in England and Wales have faced legal uncertainty for some time. Over centuries the law has evolved away from punishing cohabiting couples for fornication to largely ignoring their relationship in legal terms in modern times (Probert, 2012). The treatment of cohabitants is, however, not always consistent, and while the state recognizes the 'family' unit for some purposes, it continues to withhold the relief available to legally married couples. The most vulnerable party on the breakdown of such relationships is the economically dependent one, and this is often the woman. Calls for reform continue to be made, but little actual progress has been made.

A number of recent cases have questioned this non-recognition, including the landmark decision in *Re Brewster for Judicial Review (Northern Ireland)*[2] in which a surviving cohabitant was awarded a survivor's pension despite her deceased partner not having specifically nominated her as required by the pension conditions. A legally married partner would not have required specific nomination. At the time, it was hoped that the decision would pave the way for further recognition of the rights and needs of cohabitants and be followed by parliamentary intervention. Three years later, this is yet to materialize in any significant way.

Where religious-only marriages are concerned, the legal formalities required for state recognition and the consequences of non-recognition have been an issue attracting much debate and contestation, involving academics, divorce law practitioners, women's right activists and campaigners, politicians, policy makers and the judiciary. Each of these

2 [2017] UKSC 8.

groups encounters disparate issues arising from such relationships. Divorce law practitioners interface with clients who have no legally binding marriage, limiting their options and rights on relationship breakdown. Women's rights activists often support women who have faced abuse during their marriages, and/or face financial difficulties upon breakdown. The judiciary interfaces with marriage breakdowns where one party is seeking legal recognition to access financial resolution for jointly accumulated assets. Policy makers and politicians face appeals from activists to intervene where outcomes are unfair.

Academic discourse on the issues is expected to take a holistic view, engaging a wide range of affected parties, including those whose relationships are successful and those who voluntarily choose to be in non-legally binding marriages, in addition to those who suffer negative consequences and are denied a formal legal marriage. It is crucial to acknowledge that law reform must necessarily include consideration of all couples and individuals in religious-only marriages and not be limited to those who suffer negative outcomes. Of particular note is the correlative link between religious-only marriages and the freedom to engage in intimate relationships, as these are interdependent for religiously observant Muslim couples. Any limitation placed on entering religious marriages will have an impact on this freedom and therefore needs to be carefully balanced.

Cohabitation and religious marriage: similarities

Cohabitation manifests itself in a range of living arrangements, which may or may not be preceded by some form of ceremony, including a religious marriage. In the majority of cases, the legal outcome is the same. Where Muslim couples in particular are concerned, recent years have also seen considerable concern about the role of religious tribunals in dealing with the consequences of relationship breakdown where there is no state-recognized marriage. There are significant overlapping concerns for both cohabiting couples and those in religious-only marriages, including the lack of available and affordable legal advice for most family-related matters, which means that myths surrounding legal rights assume greater power. Cuts in legal aid remove legal options for many, while the legal routes, where available, continue to perpetuate inequality by being overly formal.

Dispute resolution forums are a key part of accessing rights, limited though they may be. Where informal dispute resolution is concerned, Sharia Councils stand accused of perpetuating gender inequality in both access to services (payment of fees by mainly women users) and the religious principles being applied. However, the financial impact of relationship breakdown for all who are considered as cohabitants is highly gendered regardless of the specific relationship type. While the imperfect and problematic Sharia Councils face a great deal of criticism, they remain an option for Muslim women. For other cohabitants, there is no equivalent informal mechanism, and the parties would have to seek legal advice and potentially pay significant costs for court proceedings to ensue.

Cohabitation and religious marriage: solutions

A number of recent reviews and proposals have sought to tackle the range of issues which arise from a lack of legal recognition of cohabitation and religious-only marriages. Solutions broadly fall within two categories: (1) amend weddings laws to facilitate simpler procedures for legal recognition, thereby encouraging more couples to legally marry; and (2) extend family law rights available to all legally recognized couples to include those in cohabiting relationships.

In 2015 the Law Commission conducted a scoping exercise, which identified a number of shortcomings in wedding laws, including the lack of rights for those in religious-only marriages, and advocated a full review of this area of law (Law Commission, 2015). The government finally agreed terms of reference for a full review in July 2019. This new review is broad, covering every stage of the process of getting married, from the legal preliminaries that are required, though the location and conduct of the ceremony, to the registration process. It will also address the legal consequences for non-compliance with legal formalities.[3] In order to assess potential solutions and reforms, it will, as usual, consider the laws in similar jurisdictions.

For example, can lessons perhaps be drawn from the wider British Isles? Scottish law authorizes celebrants 'to perform weddings as a representative of a recognised organisation, and registration is accomplished by means of a marriage schedule' (McLean, 2018: 240). Under this process, following 28 days' notice, the marriage schedule is provided to the couple to be signed and witnessed after the ceremony. The category of 'belief' marriages has been formally recognized since amendments to s 15 of the Marriage (Scotland) Act 1977 were made by the Marriage and Civil Partnership (Scotland) Act 2014. Opposite-sex couples are able to marry in a religious or belief ceremony, which must be conducted by an approved celebrant (Marriage (Scotland) Act 1977, s 8). This includes religious groups and other belief-based groups such as humanists. Scots law also allows for anyone over 21 to obtain a temporary authorization allowing them to act as a religious or belief celebrant where the person is affiliated with a religious or belief body and their proposed role as celebrant is supported by the office bearers of that body (Marriage (Scotland) Act 1977, s 12). This allows for a great deal of flexibility in who can act as celebrant for a couple, enabling friends and even family members to fulfil that role, thus facilitating personal and meaningful roles for loved ones of the couple marrying. There is also considerable flexibility regarding where a wedding

[3] See https://www.lawcom.gov.uk/law-commission-begins-work-on-weddings-reform/ (accessed 6 November 2019).

can take place, which is not limited to specific pre-approved places (Marriage (Scotland) Act 1977, s 18(a)) as amended by the Marriage and Civil Partnership (Scotland) Act 2014). The formal obligations are limited to the signing of the marriage schedule, which must be received by the district registrar within three days of the ceremony (Marriage (Scotland) Act 1977, s 15(2)).

Murray McLean has noted that it may in fact be 'individual preference' which is more salient than belief as a driver of couples' choices (2018: 238). This lends further support to proposals for a change in wedding formalities to enable couples to have personally meaningful ceremonies. Within certain groups, such as Muslim communities, there is no set ritual or archetype of religious ceremony. What the couples choose can therefore be attributed to 'individual preference'. A simpler process for entering a legally recognized marriage may increase the number of couples who engage with the process.

The particular religious beliefs and culture of Northern Ireland place it slightly out of step with the rest of the United Kingdom (Cranmer and Thompson, 2018: 302). Same-sex marriages were legislated for only in 2019, coming into force in January 2020.[4] The legal formalities for marriage are similar to Scotland, with amendments in 2003 substituting the registration of a celebrant within a register of religious officiants for the requirement for the registration of buildings.[5] It is interesting to note that the reforms were partly in response to the perceived inequality in treatment between different religious groups – 'with regard to venues, preliminary procedural requirements, authorisation of celebrants, registration requirements and hours and forms of marriage' (Cranmer and Thompson, 2018: 305). In light of historic sectarian tensions in Northern Ireland and

[4] Northern Ireland (Executive Formation etc) Act 2019, s 8.

[5] Marriage (Northern Ireland) Order 2003 (SI 2003/413).

Ireland as a whole, the need to ensure non-discriminatory provisions regarding marriage was recognized as fundamental. As such, a review in 2000 by the Law Reform Advisory Committee made a number of recommendations, including calling for civil and religious marriages to be equally valid, and the equal treatment of all religious marriages (Cranmer and Thomson, 2018: 305). While Muslim marriages were periphery considerations, advocating equality in treatment between all religious groups is clearly still a significant issue in all parts of modern-day Britain.

Reform in Northern Ireland was modelled on Scots law and provided for a wholesale change in marriage formalities. The 2003 Marriage (Northern Ireland) Order's 'main features were a new system of universal civil preliminaries to be used for all marriages, replacing the previous procedures which applied in different ways to different denominations and religions, and a relaxation of the law on civil marriage venues in order to allow people to marry in a greater variety of locations, subject to the approval of the venue by the local authority' (Cranmer and Thompson, 2018: 306). Such radical reforms are yet to be witnessed in England and Wales. In particular, the move away from registered buildings and towards a register of religious officiants provides a degree of flexibility which the current English and Welsh law lacks.

The treatment of 'belief' marriages in Northern Ireland is also complex. The contrast between religious and cultural attitudes between Northern and the Republic of Ireland can be seen most explicitly here. While the Republic of Ireland facilitates humanist and other belief marriages,[6] much like Scots law, this is not the case in Northern Ireland. In the instance of the latter, it was held in the case of *Smyth* (which

[6] Article 3 of the Civil Registration (Amendment) Act 2012 inserted article 45A into the Civil Registration Act 2004, referring specifically to secular bodies, including bodies whose 'principal objects are secular, ethical and humanist' (Article 45A(1)(b)).

was appealed to the Court of Appeal)[7] that humanist marriages may be legally formed, although not by express legal provision in the 2003 Order, but rather, by a 'loophole' in that Order. The Court of Appeal held that Article 31(3), which provides for the appointment of 'additional persons to solemnise civil marriages and carry out other functions for the purposes' of the Order, could be used to overcome any arguments of discrimination arising from Article 14 restrictions. Article 14 allows for temporary authorization to solemnize religious marriage(s), and humanism – being a belief rather than a religion – did not qualify.

Within England and Wales, two major reports were published in 2018 that are of particular relevance to the issues considered in this volume. First, *The independent review into the application of sharia law in England and Wales* concluded that there should be compelled registration for all religious marriages, an awareness campaign to ensure Muslim couples understand the outcome of such marriages, and regulation of Sharia Councils (Home Office, 2018: 17–20). These proposals have been widely criticized, and a number of the chapters in this volume (Akhtar, Parveen and Uddin) show why the Advocate-General for Scotland, Lord Keen of Elie, was quite right to describe the reference to 'civilly registering a marriage' as 'inept'.[8] Nonetheless, the Parliamentary Assembly of the Council of Europe has welcomed the proposals set out in the *Independent review* and called on the relevant authorities to implement them.[9]

---

7 *Re Smyth's Application for Judicial Review* [2017] NIQB 55; [2018] NICA 25.

8 Hansard (2019) [HL] volume 798, column 1516, available at https://hansard.parliament.uk/lords/2019-07-04/debates/942B3D60-0C64-412A-9710-4967D39CFDB6/Debate (accessed 16 March 2020).

9 Parliamentary Assembly of the Council of Europe issued 'Resolution 2253: Sharia, the Cairo Declaration and the European Convention on Human Rights' (22 January 2019), para 14. As Lord Keen pointed out, this 'does not reflect the true position of marriage law in England and Wales'.

The second report, the government's *Integrated Communities Strategy Green Paper*, identified the issue of disadvantage faced by women in religious-only marriages (MHCLG, 2018: 56), highlighting the particular detriments faced when using Sharia's Councils. The review also referred to cohabitants' misconceptions and legal protections but did not expand on this. Under the banner of 'empowering women and girls', only 'marginalised' women are focused upon, and the *Green Paper* indicated that 'the government will explore the legal and practical challenges of limited reform related to the law on marriage religious weddings' (MHCLG, 2018: 58).

In 2019 two further reports were published relating to this *Green Paper* and detailing government plans and policies – the *Integrated Communities Strategies: Summary of consultation response and Government response* (MHCLG, 2019a) and the *Integrated Communities Action Plan* (MHCLG, 2019b). The *Summary* details the results of a 12-week consultation process following publication of the *Green Paper*, involving an open online survey and a number of face-to-face consultation meetings in various British cities (MHCLG, 2019a: 6). In total, 3,400 responses in varying forms were received, the vast majority of which (3,144) were personal views.

Respondents were asked whether they agreed with the measures proposed in the *Green Paper* 'to address practices which can impact on the rights of women' (MHCLG, 2019a: 21). Individuals tended to respond negatively to this, with only 20 per cent agreeing; 61 per cent disagreed (providing a 'variety' of reasons) and 19 per cent were unsure. Interestingly, responses from organizations differed significantly, with 53 per cent agreeing, and only 11 per cent disagreeing; a further 36 per cent were not sure. The *Summary* notes that '[m]any respondents focused on religious marriage reform and suggested that this will infringe upon the rights of faith groups and shows a focus on Muslim groups' (MHCLG, 2019a: 21). Such concerns are also highlighted in a number of the chapters in this volume, including those of Akhtar,

Parveen and Naqvi. Other respondents opined that the focus should be on all women not a 'single group', and some suggested there was a need for greater 'cultural sensitivity' in addressing issues which relate to women. The government's own response did not include any comments specifically on religious-only marriages, simply stating: 'we will trial innovative approaches which address the issues identified locally and which support women in isolated communities and other marginalised groups to participate fully in society and the workplace, as well as challenge socio-cultural norms which can hold them back' (MHCLG, 2019a: 21). This can perhaps be read as an acknowledgement of the complexities of the issues, often oversimplified by campaigners and indeed the *Independent review* itself.

The subsequent *Integrated Communities Action Plan* provides a clearer idea of government policy on marriage, setting out the plan to continue to engage with key stakeholders, including faith groups, academics and lawyers, 'to test views on the policy and legal challenges of limited reform relating to the law on marriage and religious ceremonies' (MHCLG, 2019b: 18). The *Action Plan* then proposes 'work' will take place to give best effect to the policy objective. A more specific action point relates to awareness campaigns to increase knowledge about the outcome of religious-only marriages, with the *Action Plan* specifically outlining 'funding for voluntary organisations led by Register Our Marriage to roll out local targeted awareness campaigns in three areas' (MHCLG, 2019b: 19). This is clearly an appropriate short-term solution which respects individual autonomy and aligns with government responses to similar concerns of a lack of awareness of legal outcomes for all cohabiting couples.[10]

10 For example, the Living Together Campaign 2004 launched a website on the legal position of cohabiting couples, to raise awareness of the lack of legal protections. See: www.advicenow.org.uk/livingtogether (accessed 11 November 2019).

Conclusion

Modern relationship norms in contemporary England and Wales reflect a range of relationship choices. When couples enter religious-only or belief-only marriages, or choose to cohabit, the law fails to protect the resultant family units. In this England and Wales is lagging behind Scotland and the Republic of Ireland.

As cohabitants continue to be the fastest-growing family type, some form of legal response is clearly long overdue. This volume demonstrates the complex nature of the issues and bridges the conceptual gap between cohabitants and those in religious-only marriages. Bringing these issues together for the first time and exploring legal solutions to the oft-overlapping legal outcomes of these non-legally recognized relationship types, this volume proposes a range of law reform ideas. Of central concern is that legal reforms need to ensure that all vulnerable parties are equally protected and avoid situations where one group in society is treated differently from all others.

TWO

Determining the Boundaries Between Valid, Void and 'Non-Qualifying' Marriages: Past, Present and Future?

Rebecca Probert

Introduction

In recent years the question of when a marriage should be valid, when it should be categorized as void, and when it will not be recognized at all, has attracted considerable attention. Yet much of the commentary – and many of the cases – fail to engage with the precise terms of the legislation governing this area.

Understanding how the law has evolved is crucial to an appreciation of why the concept of a 'non-qualifying ceremony',[1] while unattractive to some, is nevertheless a necessary one under the current state of the law (Probert, 2013). Looking at when and why different provisions and potential grounds for invalidity were added over time also suggests ways in which the current framework might be

1 This term was proposed by the Court of Appeal in *Attorney General v Akhter and Khan* [2020] EWCA Civ 122 to replace the more controversial terminology of 'non-marriage'.

reformed to minimize the likelihood of a wedding either resulting in a void marriage or no marriage at all.

The evolution of the law

Before 1753 marriage was governed by the canon law, and the validity of a marriage depended on whether it had been conducted by an ordained Anglican clergyman (Probert, 2009a). Non-Anglican ceremonies were not afforded legal recognition. The only exception to this was the acceptance that Jewish marriages were governed by Jewish law, but this apparent privilege rested on the fact that Jewish people were regarded as legal aliens.

It is telling that there are no decisions of the ecclesiastical courts holding non-Anglican ceremonies to be void. There would have been no point in the parties litigating where the outcome was a foregone conclusion, and no advantage in obtaining a decree of nullity at a time when that conferred no rights to apply for provision. The few early 18th-century cases that did consider the rights of couples who had gone through a non-Anglican ceremony were decisions of the common law courts, which did not have the right to decide on the validity of a marriage.

Making the presence of an Anglican clergyman both necessary and sufficient was problematic in two respects. First, it meant that a marriage could be invalidated if the person who had solemnized it was not in fact ordained. Second, it meant that a marriage would be valid even if no other formal requirements had been observed. The scandal of clandestine marriages being conducted by clergymen operating out of London's Fleet prison was a key factor in prompting Parliament to put marriage on a statutory basis in 1753.

The resulting Clandestine Marriages Act 1753 focused more on compliance with specific formal requirements. Marriages celebrated after 25 March 1754 were void if they were not preceded by banns or licence, or if they were not celebrated in a church or public chapel. In addition, those marrying by licence under the age of 21 needed parental consent. Jewish and Quaker marriages were exempted.

Despite a certain degree of opposition and criticism, the Act remained in place for almost 70 years. In the 1820s, however, concern grew about the number of marriages being invalidated on the basis that one of the parties had been underage at the time of the ceremony and had not had the requisite parental consent. The fact that such marriages were usually being challenged many years after they had taken place, resulting in a number of children being bastardized, was seen as particularly problematic. After a flawed attempt at reform in 1822, the Marriage Act 1823 provided that a marriage would only be void if the parties had 'knowingly and wilfully' intermarried in any place other than a church or public chapel, or without banns or licence, or had acquiesced in that marriage being solemnized by a person who was not in Holy Orders.[2] The lack of status of the person conducting the ceremony thus once again became a factor capable of rendering the marriage void, although only in the unlikely scenario that both parties knew he was not ordained.

Thirteen years later new routes into marriage were created by the Marriage Act 1836. It introduced civil marriage and the possibility of marrying in a registered place of worship according to whatever religious rites the couple chose. Jewish and Quaker marriages were left largely untouched but were brought within the legal framework in that they now had to be preceded by civil preliminaries, along with all other non-Anglican marriages. The provision setting out when marriages would potentially be void was modelled on that in the 1823 Act, but with some key differences. Knowingly and wilfully marrying without complying with the necessary preliminaries, or in the absence of a superintendent registrar or registrar (assuming their presence was required) rendered the marriage

[2] Marriage Act 1823, s 22.

void.[3] So too would knowingly and wilfully marrying in any place other than that specified in the notice and certificate. The fact that the place in question had not been registered for marriage was not stated as affecting the validity of a marriage.

Further legislation in 1856 removed the condition that only Christian places of worship could be registered for marriage, although it was to be some decades before the first mosque was registered, and longer still before marriages could legally take place in Hindu temples and Sikh gurdwaras. The Marriage Act 1898 removed the requirement that a registrar had to be present at weddings in registered places of worship, allowing such places to appoint their own 'authorised person' to conduct the ceremony.

The inconvenience of having different types of marriages regulated by different pieces of legislation led to consolidating legislation being passed in 1949. The more fundamental problem that different types of marriages were being regulated in fundamentally different ways was left unresolved.

One final reform enacted right at the end of the 20th century should be noted. The Marriage Act 1994 enabled civil weddings to take place outside the parties' local register office for the first time. It also introduced a new ground for invalidity: that the parties had knowingly and wilfully married in a place that had not in fact been approved for the celebration of marriages.

The consequences of a void marriage

It is important to bear in mind that when the ecclesiastical courts granted a decree of nullity the practical consequences were the same as those of a non-qualifying ceremony today. The court had no power to order either party to financially support the other, and any children of the marriage were

[3] Marriage Act 1836, s 42.

illegitimate. When jurisdiction over marriage was transferred from the ecclesiastical court to the new Divorce Court in 1857, a somewhat ambiguous provision in the Matrimonial Causes Act 1857 was interpreted as allowing that court to order alimony when granting a decree of nullity, as on divorce. The fact that the Legitimacy Declaration Act 1858 gave the courts the power to make a declaration that a marriage was void – with no option of ordering alimony – suggests that the 1857 Act was misinterpreted.

Well into the second half of the 20th century there was debate about when precisely a decree of nullity could be granted, as opposed to a declaration that carried no legal consequences. The matter was finally resolved with the passage of the Family Law Act 1986, which removed the option of the court making a declaration that a marriage was void. This development meant that the only remedy available where a marriage was void for non-compliance with the formal requirements was a decree of nullity – leaving intact the court's power to make ancillary orders. In addition, the range of ancillary orders that could be made had been greatly expanded by legislation in 1970.

The necessity of a concept of 'non-qualifying' ceremony

The legislation passed in 1823 and 1836 – and consolidated in 1949 – attempted to protect individuals from a finding that their marriage was void precisely because the consequences of such a finding were so drastic, whether expressed as a decree (before 1857) or a declaration (after that date). Now, however, a finding that a marriage is void inevitably results in a decree that does have legal consequences. But when precisely can such a finding be made?

The legal status of a ceremony now depends on three elements. First, did the parties marry according to the rites of the Church of England or otherwise under the provisions of the Marriage Act? This condition prefaces the specific provisions of sections 25 and 49 of the Marriage Act 1949, which govern the validity of Anglican and non-Anglican marriages respectively. This indicates that there has to be some engagement with the terms of the Act before the question of whether the marriage might be void even arises, and that there will be some wedding ceremonies that are simply not recognized as marriages under English law.

Engagement with the terms of the Act might take a number of different forms. It might involve the couple giving notice at the register office – although in that case the likelihood of later mistakes is minimized as the registrar would offer guidance as to the next steps required. It might involve the ceremony taking place in a registered place of worship, or, potentially, in the presence of an authorized person (Probert, 2013).

It is surprising that so few of the cases in which the status of the marriage has been called into question have really engaged with the terms of the 1949 Act.[4] Asking 'whether the ceremony or event set out or purported to be a lawful marriage' and 'whether it bore all or enough of the hallmarks of marriage'[5] has little meaning unless the answers are evaluated against what the law requires. In practice, though, the courts have been reluctant to uphold marriages that do not comply with any of the requirements for a valid marriage.

There remains some ambiguity as to whether specific compliance with at least one of the formal requirements of the Act is necessary or whether it would be sufficient for the ceremony to be in a form contemplated by the legislative framework. This would not change the non-status of those

4 A notable exception is the careful judgment of Moylan J in *MA v JA and the Attorney General* [2012] EWHC 2219 (Fam), at [96] in which he noted that 'the answer to the question of when a ceremony in England is not wholly outside the provisions of the 1949 Act and will accordingly create a potentially valid marriage should be determined by reference to the provisions of the 1949 Act'. See also *Attorney General v Akhter and Khan* [2020] EWCA Civ 122.

5 See *Hudson v Leigh* [2009] EWHC 1306 (Fam).

ceremonies conducted in private houses or secular venues[6] but it would save those conducted in places of worship, regardless of whether or not that venue was registered. Judges' instinctive desire to uphold marriages conducted in places of worship is reflected in decisions such as *Chief Adjudication Officer v Bath*.[7] On this basis a ceremony such as that in *Gereis v Yagoub*,[8] which was conducted in an unregistered Coptic Orthodox Church, would be valid, at least as long as the parties had not deliberately flouted the law (Barton and Probert, 2018).

This leads on to the second and third elements that will affect the status of the marriage: whether the parties have failed to comply with any of the requirements that sections 25 and 49 identify as potentially affecting the validity of a marriage, and, if so, whether both did so 'knowingly and wilfully'. Only in cases of deliberate non-compliance will the marriage be void; as long as the marriage was within the framework of the Act an innocent failure to comply will not affect the validity of the marriage. But another way of putting this is that the court does not have the option of holding a marriage to be void if the parties did *not* 'knowingly and wilfully' fail to comply with the legal requirements. The provision in section 11 of the Matrimonial Causes Act 1973 that a marriage is only to be void in the circumstances there stated, read in conjunction with the express terms of sections 25 and 49, should preclude any such outcome.

The fact that a concept of non-qualifying ceremony is necessary does not mean that it is desirable, at least in its current form.

---

6 See, for example, *El Gamal v Al Maktoum* [2011] EWHC B27 (Fam); *Sharbatly v Shagroon* [2012] EWCA Civ 1507.

7 [2000] 1 FLR 8. In that case one basis for upholding the marriage was that the evidence that the temple was *not* registered was not strong enough to rebut the presumption that it was.

8 [1997] 1 FLR 854.

The options for reform

Simply removing the condition that a marriage would only be void if the parties had 'knowingly and wilfully' failed to comply with certain requirements would not by itself solve the issue. The obvious consequence would be that marriages would be automatically void in the circumstances set out in sections 25 and 49 of the 1949 Act. But should all of those examples of non-compliance have this effect?

It could be argued that the designation of a marriage as void rather than valid is of little practical significance. After all, the court has the same powers to reallocate property between the parties when granting a decree of nullity as it does upon divorce. In a number of cases the dispute as to the validity of the marriage emerged only when the parties were already contemplating a divorce. And if the parties are still together they have the option of going through a further, valid ceremony in any case.

Yet this rather overlooks the impact of declaring a marriage to be void. It is still a formal declaration that this particular marriage never existed in the eyes of the law and was, in the words of Nourse LJ in *Re Spence dec'd*,[9] 'only an idle ceremony [which] achieves no change in the status of the participants [and] achieves nothing of substance'.

Nor do the factors potentially rendering a marriage void under the current law reflect any coherent policy decision as to what is essential to a marriage. And these factors vary considerably between religious and civil marriages, and between different forms of religious marriages. As I have argued elsewhere, differences in whether a particular element of the process is regulated raise questions as to the necessity of that element being regulated (Probert, 2018c). If the result of non-compliance is to render a marriage

[9] [1990] Ch 652, at 661.

automatically void, those differences assume still greater significance.

Take the provisions relating to the necessity of the marriage being solemnized by a particular person. There is no statutory requirement that any specific person should conduct marriages in registered buildings, or those solemnized according to Jewish or Quaker usages. But under a scheme in which the requirements are absolute the absence of the superintendent registrar or Anglican clergy would invalidate civil marriages and those celebrated according to Anglican rites respectively.[10] In addition, questions might arise as to the status of the person who did solemnize the marriage. What if they had not been duly ordained or appointed as a superintendent registrar? Making the validity of a marriage depend upon the authorization of the person responsible for celebrating it would be to revert to the position before the Clandestine Marriages Act of 1753. The fake priest was a staple of Restoration drama for good reason, given the scope it provided for deception and doubt. The statutory framework introduced in 1753 assumed that a clergyman would conduct any marriage in the Anglican church but did not stipulate that a lack of ordination would invalidate a marriage. It was only in 1823, when the 'knowingly and wilfully' condition was introduced, that the status of the clergyman once again became relevant. And since the 'knowingly and wilfully' condition was part of the legislative framework governing civil marriage from the outset, courts have never had to decide on the status of a civil ceremony conducted by someone who was not in fact a superintendent registrar.

The place of marriage would become even more important than at present if the 'knowingly and wilfully' requirement

[10] See Marriage Act 1949, ss 49(g) and (gg) (in relation to the required presence of a superintendent registrar) and 25(3) (in relation to the person solemnizing the marriage being in Holy Orders).

were removed. Civil marriages (other than those in the register office) would be vulnerable to challenge on the basis that they had been celebrated on premises that were not approved at the time of the marriage. Given that the majority of all marriages now take place on approved premises, and the wide variety of places that can be approved, this could have a significant impact. What, for example, would be the status of a wedding celebrated at a venue that had been approved at the time notice was given but whose authorization had since lapsed? Or where the wedding took place outside the parameters of the area that had been authorized? With some fairly rudimentary structures being approved, the validity of the marriage might turn on precisely where the parties were standing at the time that the key part of the marriage ceremony took place. Even marriages within the premises of the register office might not be immune from doubt since many former marriage rooms have been redesignated as approved premises.

Similarly, Anglican weddings would be void if they had not been celebrated in 'a church or other building in which banns may be published'.[11] By contrast, there is nothing in the Act that invalidates a marriage that has been celebrated in a place of worship that has not been registered for marriage, and no requirement that Jewish or Quaker marriages take place in any particular type of venue at all.

In short, if the 'knowingly and wilfully' condition were to be removed, it would need to be combined with a paring down to the bare minimum of the forms of non-compliance that render a marriage void. Drawing on the approach in the Acts of 1753 and 1836, it is suggested that only a failure to comply with the required preliminaries should render a marriage void.

11 Marriage Act 1949, s 25(2)(a).

What should be the minimum needed for any form of legal recognition?

At the same time, lack of compliance clearly cannot be the only basis for holding a marriage to be void. There has to be some kind of ceremony for the law to designate as either valid, void or non-qualifying.

However, the law does not need to regulate the content or location of the marriage to the extent that it currently does. The legislative framework does not directly regulate the content of Anglican, Jewish or Quaker ceremonies. Nor does it regulate the location of Jewish or Quaker ceremonies, or invalidate ceremonies in a place of worship that has not been registered for marriage. The one element common to all types of marriages is that a specific person is tasked with their registration. As proposed elsewhere, a marriage should be permitted to take place anywhere if the parties have given notice and the ceremony takes place in the presence of a person responsible for registration.

Their presence would, however, be a directory rather than mandatory requirement, as would registration of the marriage itself.

Table 2.1 shows how the status of the marriage could be determined by the combination of compliance and non-compliance in any given case.

Should a simple exchange of consent suffice by itself? In *Collett v Collett*[12] this was described as being the 'essence of marriage', albeit in a context in which the parties had done rather more. But in *MA v JA and the Attorney General*[13] Moylan J rejected the idea that 'the formal exchange of voluntary consents to take one another for husband and wife' should suffice to bring a ceremony within the scope of the 1949 Act,

---

12 [1968] P 482, at 493.

13 [2012] EWHC 2219 (Fam).

Table 2.1: Suggested factors resulting in a valid, void or non-qualifying marriage

Parties gave notice	Registrar present	Marriage registered	Status
Yes	Yes	Yes	Valid
Yes	Yes	No	Valid
Yes	No	Yes	Valid
Yes	No	No	Valid
No	Yes	Yes	Void
No	Yes	No	Void
No	No	Yes	Void
No	No	No	Non-qualifying

and his objection that this could 'result in almost any form of ceremony being sufficient, wherever and however conducted'[14] applies with equal force here. Some ceremonies will inevitably continue to fall outside the legal framework.

Conclusion

It is clear that the issue of when a marriage should be void cannot be solved by judicial interpretation, however creative, or by a minor change to the legislation. The implications for every part of the process of getting married need to be thought through. At the time of writing, the Law Commission is carrying out a full review of the law governing weddings and it will be vital for it to give careful consideration to the circumstances in which a marriage will be valid, void or non-qualifying.

14 [2012] EWHC 2219 (Fam), at [93].

THREE

'Cohabitants' in the Law of England and Wales: a Brief Introduction

Joanna Miles

Introduction

A primary focus of this book is the legal treatment of couples in informal relationships, who have married under a religious law or in a personalized ceremony not recognized by the state, or who are cohabiting without a ceremony. As Rebecca Probert's chapter explains, some of those who have gone through a ceremony will have marriages that are classed as 'void', which for many legal purposes – perhaps counter-intuitively – gives rise to similar, and usually identical, consequences to valid marriages. But in other situations, while some of these couples may regard themselves as married – at least for religious, cultural or psychological purposes – they will be regarded by English law as having a 'non-qualifying ceremony'. Such couples may (mistakenly) assume that their marriage is recognized by the state and conduct their lives accordingly. Paradoxical though it may appear, English law will treat couples in these 'non-qualifying ceremony' cases just as it would treat couples who live together but who are clearly not married in any sense, including couples who have deliberately decided not to marry precisely because they do not want the legal and cultural consequences of marriage.[1] All these couples are commonly referred to in the UK as 'cohabitants'; in some other jurisdictions, such as Australia and New Zealand, they have a 'de facto relationship' – that is to say, one that exists and is recognized in fact but not in law ('de jure').

The place of cohabitation in families in the UK today

Marriage remains the principal basis of family life in the UK: in 2017, two thirds of the 19 million 'families' (defined as couples with or without dependent children and lone parents living with a child) were based on marriage or civil partnership (ONS, 2017a). However, in 2015 the marriage rate (that is to say, the number of people marrying per thousand unmarried people aged 16+ in the population) was at its lowest since calculations began in 1862 (ONS, 2018c). Meanwhile, cohabitation is the fastest-growing family type. There were 3.4 million cohabiting couple families in the UK in 2018, of which 1.3 million had dependent children (ONS, 2019). Nearly half of all births involve mothers who are not married, and just under a third of all births are registered by parents who are living together unmarried (ONS, 2017).

Finding the law related to cohabitants: which couples?

What does the law have to say about this growing family form? Unfortunately, there is no quick or straightforward answer – no 'one-stop-shop' of rules about cohabiting couple relationships. Instead, we have to go hunting in various corners of the law in search of rights, duties and other legal provisions that apply to these relationships. That task is made no easier by the fact that the law has no uniform terminology for referring to these relationships.

1 For these purposes, all references to marriage include civil partnership, which from the end of 2019 has been available to all couples, whatever their gender. Couples who do not marry or register a civil partnership are treated by law in the same way, again, regardless of their gender.

Many Acts of Parliament refer to couples who 'live together as if they were husband and wife'[2] or 'as if they were civil partners'.[3] Applying this concept, of course, requires us to have a view about what living arrangements are marriage-like – and about what 'living together' entails. The standard test comes from a case decided in 1982 in the context of welfare benefits law,[4] in which Mr Justice Woolf adopted a set of six 'signposts' to be used to help decide if a relationship is marriage-like:

- membership of the same household;
- the stability of the relationship;
- the existence of financial support or interdependence between the parties;
- the existence of a sexual relationship between the parties;
- the presence of children in their household;
- public acknowledgement of the parties' relationship as being that of a couple.

Not all of these factors need to be present – in particular, a couple can clearly have a marriage-like relationship without having children. But legislation applying to cohabitants generally requires them to be living together – that is to say, living in the same household – and that means that they need to have a shared domestic life together – a shared centre of gravity – even if they do not both live full time in the same house or in just one house.[5] Couples who live separately will not be considered to be 'living together'.

2 Despite the use of 'husband and wife', such provisions are now to be read as referring equally to same-sex couples: Marriage (Same Sex Couples) Act 2013, Sch 3, para 2.

3 For example, the Inheritance (Provision for Family and Dependants) Act 1975, as amended, s 1(1A) and (1B).

4 *Crake v Supplementary Benefits Commission* [1982] 1 All ER 498.

5 See *Kotke v Saffarini* [2005] EWCA Civ 221.

By contrast, some newer Acts of Parliament have used relationship concepts that do not obviously require couples to be cohabiting in that sense. For example, civil law remedies to prevent molestation may now be made between members of 'intimate personal relationship[s] … of significant duration'.[6] And 'two people … living as partners in an enduring family relationship' (excluding certain blood relationships) can apply together to adopt a child or for a parental order following a surrogacy arrangement.[7] It has been decided that this test does not require the partners to live *together* in the same household.[8] On their face, at least some of these tests could apply to purely platonic relationships.

What do cohabitants get where they are legally recognized?

So, English law has various ways of referring to the sort of couple relationships that this book is concerned with. But the recognition by English law of these relationships is relatively limited: both in the sense that such relationships are recognized for some legal purposes but not others, and in the sense that, where they are recognized, the legal consequences ascribed to those relationships are commonly less intensive than those attaching to their formal counterparts.

The law relating to children

In one large and important area of family law, couples' relationships are treated largely identically, regardless of the form of their relationship: that relating to children. As noted previously, unmarried couples can become parents together

6 Family Law Act 1996, s 62(3)(ea).

7 See Adoption and Children Act 2002, s 144(4)–(7); Human Fertilisation and Embryology Act 2008, s 54(2)(c).

8 *T and M v OCC and C* [2010] EWHC 964.

via adoption and surrogacy, and using assisted reproductive technologies.[9] More generally, the law no longer differentiates between children based on whether their birth was 'legitimate', that is to say, whether they were born to parents who were married.[10] All parents have equal status in the law and are equally entitled to acquire 'parental responsibility' for their children. The one (quite significant) difference is that, while all mothers and all fathers who are married to the mother acquire parental responsibility for their children automatically, a father who is not married to the mother will only acquire parental responsibility if he is registered as the father on the child's birth certificate, or if he reaches a formal agreement with the mother or obtains a court order.[11] But even this difference has relatively little impact in practice as the birth certificates of over 95 per cent of children record the names of both parents (ONS, 2017). Importantly, financial obligations owed by parents to their children apply regardless of the nature of the parents' relationship (and regardless of whether both parents have parental responsibility) – so child support law applies between formerly cohabiting parents just as it does between divorced spouses,[12] and the courts also have the power to order other financial remedies for the benefit of children under legislation very similar to that which applies on divorce.[13]

The criminal law

Family relationships matter for some criminal law purposes. The familial child sex offences in the Sexual Offences Act 2003 take a very broad view of 'family' for these purposes,

---

[9] Human Fertilisation and Embryology Act 2008, ss 36–38, 43–45.

[10] Family Law Reform Act 1987.

[11] Children Act 1989, s 4.

[12] Child Support Act 1991, as amended.

[13] Children Act 1989, Sch 1; compare similar powers to benefit children under the Matrimonial Causes Act 1973, Part II.

covering unmarried as well as marital and other familial relationships.[14] By contrast, only spouses and civil partners are protected by the antiquated rule that it is impossible to commit the criminal offence of conspiracy where the only conspirators are the spouses/civil partners.[15] And unmarried partners are not covered by the rules that exempt spouses and civil partners from being compelled to testify against each other.[16]

Tax and benefits law

The legal recognition of cohabitants in their financial relationship with the state is again uneven, with the result that, overall, they come out worse than spouses. Cohabitants are treated *just like* spouses – as an economic unit – for the purpose of calculating means-tested benefits,[17] with the result that they are entitled together to less than they would be entitled to individually. This is designed to ensure that couples have no incentive to cohabit without marrying in order to increase their income from public funds. And yet in the taxation context, they are disadvantaged by being treated *differently* from spouses: notably, they are denied access to the 100 per cent exemption from inheritance tax enjoyed by the surviving spouse and the – considerably less valuable – income tax marriage allowance.[18]

---

14 Sexual Offences Act 2003, ss 25–27.

15 Criminal Law Act 1977, s 2(2)(a), as amended.

16 Police and Criminal Evidence Act 1984, s 80.

17 For example, Social Security Contributions and Benefits Act 1992, ss 124, 134, 136–7; and, for Universal Credit, see https://www.gov.uk/government/publications/universal-credit-and-couples-an-introduction/universal-credit-further-information-for-couples [accessed 6 June 2019].

18 See https://www.gov.uk/marriage-allowance [accessed 6 June 2019].

Property and finances when one partner dies

Interestingly, cohabitants receive quite extensive legal recognition where one partner dies. Admittedly, this is less generous than that for widowed spouses, in that a surviving cohabitant is not automatically entitled to inherit from their partner's estate if the partner dies without a will ('intestate'). However, the survivor will be entitled to succeed to certain types of tenancies over rental property that the deceased held.[19] If the deceased partner died as a result of someone else's fault in an accident, the survivor can sue for compensation, provided they had been cohabiting for at least two years immediately preceding the death. And the same surviving cohabitant can apply to the court for financial provision from their deceased partner's estate, whether the partner died with or without a will, where the result of the will – or of the intestacy rules – does not give the survivor 'reasonable financial provision' for their maintenance.[20] Whether, and if so how much, provision will be made for the survivor in such a case is a matter of discretion and depends on all the circumstances of the case, including the situation of other individuals who either have been provided for from the estate already or who are also making a claim. But whatever provision is made can only be for the surviving partner's 'maintenance' or needs – by contrast, the provision for a widowed spouse can extend beyond what they need to maintain themself.

Property and finances if the couple separates

The difference in treatment of cohabitants and spouses is most stark and well known on relationship breakdown.

[19] For example, Rent Act 1977, Sch 1, para 2(2).

[20] Inheritance (Provision for Family and Dependants) Act 1975, as amended.

When spouses divorce, the court has extensive powers to distribute all the spouses' income and property, including pensions, between them in order to achieve an overall outcome that is 'fair'.[21] 'Fairness' for these purposes is measured in various ways and depends on the circumstances of the individual case. But the underlying principles rest on three central ideas of marriage: (1) an equal partnership that entitles the spouses to share equally in core marital assets (whoever paid for them), in particular the family home and whatever they acquired during the marriage other than by way of a gift made to one of them or something that one of them inherited; (2) an interdependent relationship in which the spouses assume responsibility to meet each other's needs, particularly needs that are generated by their contributions to the marriage; and (3), building on that last idea, ensuring that whichever spouse was more economically disadvantaged by their contributions to the marriage should not shoulder that burden alone on divorce, whether or not they are in financial need. The court can make various types of order, including orders for particular assets to be transferred from one spouse to the other; or for an asset to be sold and the proceeds of sale shared; or for a pension fund to be shared; or for one party to make regular payments of income to the other.

None of this applies to cohabitants. The financial remedies that exist for the benefit of any of the couple's children apply, including child support, but only for joint children of the couple – previously cohabiting 'step-parents' have no legal responsibility for their ex-partner's children. But the only power that the court has to adjust their property rights on separation that is akin to remedies available on divorce is where the couple rented their home: the court can then transfer the tenancy from the joint names of both to just one of them, or

---

21 Matrimonial Causes Act 1973, Part II and related case law, in particular *Miller, McFarlane* [2006] UKHL 24.

a tenancy held by one partner to the other. That aside, there are no financial remedies available between the ex-partners themselves for *their* benefit, rather than for the benefit of the children. So there is no question of a court ordering one ex-partner to transfer property to the other, or to share a pension, or to make regular maintenance payments.

So when cohabitants separate, their financial and property disputes have to be dealt with primarily through the law of property: the simple question is 'who owns what?' and the court is only concerned to answer that question, not to consider who *should* get what, applying any sort of 'fairness' consideration of the sort that applies on divorce. The sorts of outcomes that the law of property will generate will vary depending on particular features of the case. Whether those outcomes achieve anything like the equal sharing, provision for needs, and compensation for economic disadvantages that divorcing spouses enjoy will be quite fortuitous because none of those principles is of itself relevant to the court's decision. And there can be no question of any regular payments of income (other than child support) or of sharing pensions. The main focus of attention will commonly be on the family home. Some of the property law principles that apply to homes are quite complicated both to describe and to apply, but in short:[22]

- If the couple owned the property in joint names – this will involve both of them having their name on the entry for the property at Land Registry – then they will probably both have a stake in it.
- The form on which the couple registered their purchase of the property with Land Registry should state how they share it – either as 'joint tenants' (in which case they own it 50:50) or in some other specified shares.

[22] The leading cases are *Stack v Dowden* [2007] UKHL 17, *Jones v Kernott* [2011] UKSC 53 and *Lloyds Bank v Rosset* [1991] 1 AC 107.

- If the couple did not record on that form or elsewhere in suitably formal, signed writing how they own the property, then trusts law has to be used to work out what shares each of the two owners have, if any.
- Similarly, if the property is registered in the name of just one of them, then trusts law will have to be used to work out whether the other person has any share in the value of the property at all and if so how big that share is.
- Those trusts law principles primarily ask: whether the parties shared a common intention that they should share the property's value; and whether the party seeking a greater share than 50 per cent (in a joint-owners case) or any share (in a sole-owner case) can show that they have relied on that shared intention to their detriment. If the person seeking to claim a (bigger) share cannot prove an express conversation or exchange of correspondence which made this clear, then they will need to try to find other conduct from which the court will feel able – on the balance of probabilities – to infer that they had such a shared intention. But the case law indicates that the courts will rarely if ever feel able to infer an intention in that way other than where the party seeking the (bigger) share has made a financial contribution to the purchase of the house, including by helping to pay any mortgage.
- If that can be shown, then the last question is what intention, if any, the parties had about how big their respective shares should be – and if they had no intention about that, the court will take its own view about what shares would be fair. It is not clear at this very last stage how the court approaches 'fairness' but what is clear is that they are not applying that concept in the same way that they do in divorce cases, discussed previously.

That is only the barest outline of a detailed and complex area of law. If the couple specify how they own the property when they buy it, then all is straightforward. The problems arise when they do not do that, which will be most common where the property is owned in the name of just one of them. The main points to notice about the law outlined here are that:

- it is all backward looking: that is to say, it is concerned to establish what was said, agreed and done in the past – unlike the law that applies on divorce, it is not interested in who needs what to live going forward;
- it prioritizes conversations and intentions specifically about property *ownership*: it is not concerned with broader intentions about sharing a *home*; and
- it prioritizes people who make financial contributions over those whose contributions to family life are purely 'domestic': in a divorce case, those contributions would be valued equally, but in this area of law, they get you nowhere by themselves, and there are no compensatory principles concerned to make good losses arising from sacrifices made for the good of the family.

Judges and others have been calling for reform of this area of the law for decades. The government's law reform body, the Law Commission, examined the area in depth (Law Commission, 2006, 2007) but the government has not decided to implement its recommendations, even though very similar laws have now been operating in Scotland for more than ten years.[23]

Conclusion

Cohabiting couples in English law exist in a sort of halfway house: recognized for some legal purposes, but not others. The fact that they are recognized in *some* legal contexts may be what fuels the so-called 'common law marriage myth' – the mistaken idea, held by a very large minority of British adults, that simply by living together as a couple for a given number

[23] Family Law (Scotland) Act 2006.

of years, you are treated as if you are married (see Barlow, this volume). While that is true in some areas of law, it is not true in others – most importantly, if the relationship ends in separation. And that can give rise to financial hardship for economically weaker individuals. That outcome may seem most unfair in those cases where one or both of the couple honestly believed that they were married, but where the ceremony that they participated in failed to create a marriage recognized – even as a void marriage – in English law.

FOUR

Modern Marriage Myths: the Dichotomy Between Expectations of Legal Rationality and Lived Law

Anne Barlow

Introduction

Today, few social distinctions are made between those who cohabit rather than marry or enter into a civil partnership. Yet the law in England and Wales continues to draw a sharp distinction between formal and informal couple relationships, particularly on relationship breakdown or the death of a partner. In so doing, the law assumes that people are 'legally rational' and that a conscious and informed choice is being made by couples exercising their autonomy with full knowledge of the legal differences between these functionally similar relationships. Yet how realistic an assumption is this, and how far should such assumptions be permitted to influence the family law reform agenda?

Drawing on nationally representative research from the British Social Attitudes survey conducted in 2018, which demonstrates that, despite public information campaigns, the 'common law marriage myth', whereby people falsely believe that cohabitation gives the same legal rights as marriage, is alive and well, this chapter will first consider the flaws in the assumption that couples are making an informed choice and the implications for family law and policy. It will go on to suggest that another dimension to this myth has recently been exposed which reinforces the need for caution in assuming that conscious, mutual and autonomous choices are always being made. This aspect involves a discussion of a further category of couples who are treated in law as 'cohabitants' yet who may similarly be unaware of their different legal status. Unlike informal cohabiting couples, these couples have actually gone through a religious ceremony of marriage in England and Wales but have failed to comply with the formalities required by law.[1] This is a situation most common among (but not exclusive to) Muslim couples marrying in England and Wales. While on the face of it, informal cohabitants and those in religious-only marriages are unlikely to share attitudes on the importance of marriage, many of them do share not only a common fate in terms of how the law views their relationships, but also a belief that the law either does or ought to recognize their unions and provide family law protection automatically, given their accepted and normalized family practices and lived experience or 'lived law'.

The arrival of opposite-sex civil partnerships, introduced in 2019,[2] now adds urgency to the question of whether cohabitants are making a conscious choice to opt out. Opposite-sex civil partnerships have been presented as a solution for cohabiting couples, implicitly rendering redundant the need for further cohabitation law reform. This chapter will consider the current evidence as to whether civil partnerships are likely to be sufficient to meet the needs of those who are cohabiting.

The common law marriage myth problem and 'lived law'

Socially, the type of couple relationship people enter into is seen as a matter of personal choice. As these choices

1 These are principally contained in the Marriage Act 1949 as amended.

2 Civil Partnerships, Marriages and Deaths (Registration etc) Act 2019.

expand or shift, a common belief based on lived experience emerges that the law will reflect what have become normal family behaviours. So, as more couples partner and parent as cohabitants and are accepted as such without stigmatization, the more people will expect that the law both ought to and indeed does recognize such a common family form, irrespective of how the law has actually responded (Duncan et al, 2005). As Simon Duncan explains, '[i]n their eyes they are as good as married already given the "lived law" of everyday life in everyday institutions like schools, workplaces or hospitals where cohabitation is equated with marriage' (Duncan, 2011: para 2.09).

This may go some way to explaining the endurance of the common law marriage myth and the difficulties in dispelling it. Statistics show that cohabiting families are the fastest-growing family type in Britain. There were 3.4 million cohabiting couples in the UK in 2018, more than doubling from the 1.5 million recorded in 1996 (ONS, 2019). Fifteen per cent of dependent children in England and Wales live in cohabiting couple families. The de-stigmatization and normalization of doing family life in this way has seen the social imperatives for formal marriage greatly reduce both before and after a couple have children. Added to this is the fact that cohabitation is recognized by the state as equivalent to marriage in some (relatively few) areas of law. During a relationship, cohabiting couples are treated as if they are married for the purpose of means-tested welfare benefits for example (Miles, this volume). This, in turn, it is suggested, then acts to reinforce the false understanding of the law's approach to such families in other contexts, embedding the 'lived law' experience as truth in people's minds despite the fact that they are not consistently treated as married in other areas of law.

The extent of belief in the existence of 'common law marriage' was first tested empirically in 2000. Using the nationally representative British Social Attitudes (BSA) survey published in 2001,[3] it was established that there was a common law marriage myth phenomenon. Over half of people in England and Wales (56 per cent) falsely believed that couples who lived together for a period of time had a common law marriage which gave them the same rights as married couples. Among opposite-sex cohabitants themselves, the population actually affected, this belief rose to 60 per cent (Barlow et al, 2001).

This evidence was at the time considered a shocking revelation and led to revisions of government material such as social security leaflets that used the phrase 'common law marriage' as a term to describe cohabitation in order to avoid endorsing the myth. In addition, there was a determination at a policy level to address the problem and a government-funded public information campaign was launched to counter the myth. This took the form of The Living Together Campaign (LTC), which aimed to ensure that cohabiting couples were better informed by virtue of a high-profile publicity campaign using a range of media (Barlow et al, 2007). It gave free access to materials that explained the legal differences between marriage and cohabitation and enabled couples to make 'living together agreements' and wills, with free downloadable forms, checklists and documents based on accurate legal information.[4] Yet the hope that legal awareness would be significantly increased was dashed when further research, undertaken in 2006–7, found that improvements in awareness were only marginal. The findings revealed that the majority of people (51 per cent) as well as the majority of cohabitants (53 per cent) still believed in the common law marriage myth (Barlow et al, 2008). The LTC had sown some seeds of doubt about the

[3] Full details of the survey methodology are set out in Barlow et al, 2001. The survey was based on an England and Wales sample of n=2669.

[4] The Advicenow website still exists – see https://www.advicenow.org.uk/living-together. However, there is now a charge for some of its materials.

effects of cohabitation[5] but had not managed to debunk the myth (Barlow et al, 2007). Rather, the idea that cohabitation gave rights equivalent to marriage after a period of time was still embedded in the public understanding. In 2018, some ten years on, this issue was revisited. It was anticipated that there would be a significant decline in the number believing in the common law marriage myth, given the sustained media focus on this issue[6] over the previous decade as the work of the Law Commission (Law Commission, 2007), key court decisions,[7] and successive Private Member's Bills[8] ensured that the topic was never far from the headlines. Yet findings from the most recent BSA survey[9] showed this was not in fact the case (Albakri et al, 2019). As illustrated in Table 4.1, while there has been some decline in the number of believers, almost half of the population (46 per cent) still explicitly agree with the statement that 'couples who live together for a period of time have a common law marriage which gives them the same rights as married couples'. Many people therefore remain ignorant of the fact that from a legal perspective there are significant differences between the legal treatment of cohabiting and married couples. Worryingly, the data also show that belief in

5 The number of respondents who were unsure whether or not cohabiting couples did have marriage equivalence in legal terms rose from 6 to 10 per cent.

6 See, for example, Resolution's campaign information and 2017 video at http://www.resolution.org.uk/Campaign_Resources/.

7 Examples are *Stack v Dowden* [2007] UKHL 17; *Jones v Kernott* [2011] UKSC 53; *Gow v Grant* [2012] UKSC 29; *McLaughlin, Re Judicial Review (Northern Ireland)* [2018] UKSC 48; *Brewster, Judicial Review* [2017] UKSC 8; Langford *v Secretary of State for Defence* [2019] EWCA Civ 1271.

8 From the Cohabitation Rights Bill 2008–9 to the Cohabitation Rights Bill 2017–19.

9 The common law marriage myth question asked in the BSA survey undertaken during the 2018 fieldwork repeated the wording used in 2000 and 2006. It was commissioned by the University of Exeter and funded by the Economic and Social Research Council. For this survey, n=2111.

Table 4.1: Public belief in 'common law marriage' 2000–18

Do unmarried couples have a common law marriage?, 2000–2018, England and Wales			
Base: respondents in England and Wales	2000 %	2006 %	2018 %
Definitely/probably do	56	51	46
Definitely/probably do not	37	37	41
Unweighted base	2699	2514	2105
Weighted base	2731	2513	2111

Source: NatCen's British Social Attitudes survey 2018.

the myth rises to 55 per cent among those households with children in both the cohabiting and married parent groups. Question wording:

> As far as you know, do unmarried couples who live together for some time have a 'common law marriage' which gives them the same legal rights as married couples?

The significance of these findings for the take-up of opposite-sex civil partnerships will be considered further in the following section but the embedded nature of the myth and the spectrum of reasons for cohabiting rather than marrying may challenge its potential efficacy.

Before examining these motivation issues, let us now turn to the Muslim marriage myth situation.

Muslim marriage myths: another 'lived law' problem?

Within the Muslim community, there is a significant trend towards *nikah*-only marriages in England and Wales. In such cases, couples marry each other in a ceremony that is recognized as religiously valid but which does not constitute a legally valid marriage in the law of England and Wales unless the requisite legal formalities are also observed. This disconnect between the religious ceremony and its legal validity disproportionately affects the Muslim community since Islamic marriages are not customarily performed in places of worship registered for marriage under the Marriage Act 1949. If the couple have also failed to give notice, this typically results in the union being classified in the case law as what is now termed a 'non-qualifying ceremony'[10] and not even a void marriage, which would give stronger rights and remedies for financial provision in the case of relationship breakdown (see Probert, 2013, and this volume).

This situation leaves many religiously married Muslim couples regarded in law as cohabitants. As yet, there is no robust and clear research evidence about the extent to which either or both parties to such marriages are aware of the inferior status of their marriage in the eyes of the law. However, some indication can be gained from a 2017 survey of over 900 Muslim women in 14 British cities undertaken for a Channel 4 documentary. While some caution must be exercised, this found that 61 per cent of their sample had contracted traditional *nikah*-only marriages without completing the legal formalities. This was despite over three quarters of them reporting that they wanted their marriages to be recognized in UK law (True Vision, 2017). The programme highlighted some cases where this had resulted in a lack of access to the family courts, where an equal division of the couple's assets would have been the starting point; instead, the financially weaker party had the expense of making a claim using trust law to prove an interest in the family home (see Miles, this volume).

Perhaps surprisingly, an increase in the popularity of *nikah*-only weddings has been observed by some Islamic

10 Following *Attorney General v Akhter and Khan* [2020] EWCA Civ 122.

law practitioners. One such specialist, Aina Khan, launched a campaign, Register Our Marriage,[11] in 2012 to make it compulsory for all religious marriages to be registered. While this campaign message was misguided as it is not registration but a legally binding ceremony that is required, the work of the campaign did also highlight the scale of the problem. In 2017 it reported that more than 100,000 people in the UK do not have legally recognized marriages, and more than 90 per cent of mosques were not registering religious marriages under civil law, increasing the numbers who are treated as cohabitants in law.

The increase in religious-only marriages as a growing cultural norm has resonance with the 'lived law' behaviours of cohabiting couples. When people marry, they tend not to be thinking about their situation on divorce or bereavement. Those who are religious are likely to value the religious recognition of their marriage above that of the law. It seems likely that these factors combine to make one or both parties in many situations, in so far as they think about it at all, regard the need for legal formalities or an additional ceremony as unnecessary. This chimes with Simon Duncan's conclusions in relation to his study of unmarried couples: '[i]n all these examples we find people usually making family decisions pragmatically, with reference to relationships, social norms, "lived law", and the presumptions of particular social groups in different places' (Duncan, 2011: para 2.11).

This type of decision making does not usually become problematic until the relationship breaks down or one partner dies. One view is that if people are choosing to ignore legal formalities which give them rights and remedies in these situations, the law need do no more. Yet is this really an active choice and should family law limit its rights and remedies to those who are legally rational about their family life?

11 See further https://www.registerourmarriage.org/

How should the law respond?

The view of the Law Commission for England and Wales was that reform was needed both in relation to financial remedies on relationship breakdown and on the death of a partner (Law Commission 2007, 2011). It proposed a system on separation which did not place cohabitation on a par with marriage (in contrast to the situation in Australia and New Zealand). Eligible cohabitants would have been able to apply for a financial remedy as long as they had not mutually agreed to opt out. A remedy would not have been automatic, but instead aimed at redressing relationship-generated economic advantage or disadvantage. This was very broadly in line with the Family Law (Scotland) Act 2006, which provides such remedies to Scottish cohabitants.[12]

Other jurisdictions, such as the Netherlands or France, provide an opt-in approach. Dutch registered partnerships are equivalent to marriage, while the French Pacte Civil de Solidarité (PaCS') offers what are sometimes termed 'marriage-lite' family law rights and remedies. In both jurisdictions, some very limited automatic rights relating to, for example, tenancy succession of the family home also apply to cohabiting couples who have not registered.

In essence, the recent extension of civil partnership to opposite-sex couples in England and Wales as implemented in December 2019 follows the Dutch opt-in marriage-mirror model. But how far will this resolve the issues with cohabitation law as it currently stands?

---

[12] At the time of writing the 2006 Act is under review with a view to extending the rights of cohabitants. The Scottish Law Commission is revisiting Scots cohabitation law as part of its Tenth Programme of Law Reform: https://www.scotlawcom.gov.uk/law-reform/law-reform-projects/aspects-of-family-law/. The Scottish Government is in the process of reviewing the rights on death of cohabitants as part of its 2019 consultation on the law of succession – see https://www.gov.scot/publications/consultation-law-succession/pages/4/

It is suggested that the answer to this lies within the motivations and beliefs of the majority of cohabiting couples. As we have seen, the common law marriage myth is still widespread, particularly among cohabitants with children. There is some evidence that this deters people from marrying and would seem therefore likely without more to deter future civil partnering on the same grounds. As one of the research participants 'in a previous study I led with Simon Duncan and Grace James commented in 2002: 'Well, what's the point of getting married because we're classed as though we're married – we're living together and if we do split up we still do what a married couple would do – split everything, kids, responsibility and everything' (Duncan et al, 2012: 386). While the BSA survey in 2018 confirmed that the move to equal civil partnership is a popular reform, with over two thirds (65 per cent of all respondents rising to 71 per cent of cohabitants) agreeing that this should be available to opposite-sex couples as an alternative to marriage (Albakri et al, 2019: 5–9), a typology of cohabitants drawn from combining data from two of my other studies undertaken with Carol Burgoyne and Janet Smithson in 2006-7 provides further insight into similarities between those in religious-only marriages and the wider cohabiting population. Critically, it also informs the likely reactions to opposite-sex civil partnership and the need for any further legal response.

Using the typology

Carol Smart and Pippa Stevens' earlier work had suggested that cohabitants are based along a spectrum from the contingently committed to the mutually committed (Smart and Stevens, 2000), which challenged the need for cohabitant rights writ large. For if cohabiting couples did not exhibit the same commitment and stability as married couples it was easier to dismiss the need for marriage-like regulation. Our typology aimed to look at this spectrum in a different way and in more depth in the context of how likely couples were to respond to legal knowledge about their situation (Barlow and Smithson, 2010: 335–42). We identified four overlapping groups of cohabitants, which seem also to map onto those in religious-only marriages as follows:

- Ideologues – who reject (legal) marriage on ideological grounds;
- Romantics – those who believe in the relationship and that all will be well in both groups;
- Pragmatists – both parties unaware of their legal situation but will marry (or enter into a civil partnership) once aware;
- Uneven couples – one party aware and one in ignorance, where power not evenly spread.

In terms of those in religious-only marriages, it seems unlikely that the introduction of equal civil partnership will be an attractive option, given its initial incarnation as a same-sex institution. This reform on its own will leave this group in the same vulnerable situation.

In terms of the wider group of cohabitants, it is suggested that equal civil partnership will only be attractive to a relatively small group, again not resolving the problem for the vast majority. Drawing on our two samples of opposite-sex cohabitants interviewed in 2006–7, the Ideologues will undoubtedly embrace civil partnership. Indeed the couple who challenged the current law in the courts, Rebecca Steinfeld and Charles Keiden,[13] expressed the views of many of our ideological couples about wanting to avoid the patriarchal nature of the institution of marriage. However, only 10 per cent of our national sample, as compared to 33 per cent of those who had visited the LTC website, were put in this Ideologue group. Pragmatists, Romantics and Uneven couples each constituted

[13] *R (ota Steinfeld and Keidan) v Secretary of State for International Development (in substitution for the Home Secretary and the Education Secretary)* [2018] UKSC 32.

approximately 30 per cent of the national sample of opposite-sex cohabitants. Some of the Pragmatists will lean towards being Ideologues and others towards being Romantics, and will, once they become legally aware, either enter into a civil partnership or marry. However, if they are common law marriage myth believers – and some of them certainly will be – they will do neither. Romantics, similarly, are often common law marriage myth believers. A few may enter into a civil partnership but the majority are keen to marry once they can afford a 'proper wedding' and so are likely to prefer to wait to marry, given the requirements are the same for both.

However, equal civil partnership does not assist the Uneven couples. To either marry or enter into a civil partnership both have to agree to that course of action. Where such couples hold differing views on formalizing their relationship or where one perceives it as in their interests to do so and the other does not, then no progress can be made. This group alone constitute some 30 per cent of cohabitants, but they are often couples who have cohabited for long periods and who have had children together.

Conclusion

Using this typology as a framework for analysis, and bearing in mind that almost half of all cohabitants believe in the common law marriage myth, it is concluded that opposite-sex civil partnership is a remedy for the few not the many. It is of course an excellent vehicle for couples who are both ideologically opposed to marriage and are legally aware, and is a welcome addition to family law institutions. However, at best only around a half of those who do not believe in the common law marriage myth – so roughly a quarter of the total cohabiting population – are likely to consider civil partnership given their motivations for cohabitation. This view is a best estimate based on our 2006–7 data and taking account of the slight decline in myth believers in the 2018 BSA survey. As we have seen some, if not much, improvement in the rates of legal awareness, this is likely to have resulted in an increase in ideological couples since 2008. It is difficult to know how many Pragmatists will prefer civil partnership to marriage but this could be around half, so 15 per cent. A few but not many Romantics may take this route as civil partnership is not a marriage-lite option and typically they are committed to marrying in style in the future, rather than seeking a formal alternative to marriage. This leaves three quarters either unaware of their situation or unable to do anything about it where their partner does not agree to take action.

While some of these cohabiting couples will be happy with their situation and are actively choosing a relationship with no legal implications, from our earlier research this is not the majority. The recent BSA survey, while showing some inroads into the myth, suggests this change is far too small to leave the law as it stands. As we have seen, myths are embedded when they are confirmed by social practices. For the majority of cohabitants, the assumption of legal protection is one that is difficult to shift given the way it is consistent with lived law experiences within the community and, in the case of those in religious-only marriages, their 'higher' values. This renders legal rationality around family practices, as desirable as it may be, counter-intuitive and difficult to achieve.

Thus despite the rhetoric around cohabitation as a mutual and autonomous couple choice, it seems that a functional approach to cohabitation law is still needed if family law is to continue to protect the vulnerable in today's more varied couple relationships, where relationship-generated disadvantage is itself more of a reality than a myth.

FIVE

The Case for Moving Away from 'Non-Marriage' Declarations

Vishal Vora

Introduction

Marriage is an important milestone in anyone's life. British South Asian communities in particular continue to hold marriage as an almost mandatory requirement, despite the increasing trend of cohabitation in wider British society. Cohabitation for the vast majority of self-classifying observant Muslims is neither permitted nor accepted under any circumstances, at least in a public and open form. This is chiefly because Islam prohibits adultery and restricts sexual relationships to within the framework of marriage. In order for a British Muslim couple to live together, they must marry in a form that is accepted by their community. It is important to state that this requirement also comes from the individuals themselves as marriage provides them the opportunity to remember and reaffirm their commitment to traditions and beliefs. Legal difficulties arise in those few cases where the marriage entered into does not comply with the law. Sometimes, but not always, this is a wilful failure, usually on behalf of one party.

Background

Marriage law was first put on the statute books in 1753 (Clandestine Marriages Act) and has sought to provide when and how a marriage will be deemed valid or void. The question of proving whether someone is married or not has been around for a long time but with better record keeping, this issue had mostly disappeared. However, over the past two decades or so, the question has arisen frequently for British Muslim couples, typically but not exclusively when the wife applies for divorce and financial orders. At this point the husband will often defend the petition on the basis that there was no valid legal marriage under the law of England and Wales and that the ceremony they underwent was merely religious in nature.

A failure to comply with the formalities required by English law may result in a marriage being classified as valid, void or a non-qualifying[1] ceremony. The differences between the classifications are important for any party seeking financial relief. Essentially the first two will result in claims for financial relief but a finding of a non-qualifying ceremony will prevent any such application. In this situation, if the facts allow, an application can be made to resolve disputes about the ownership of property with reference to the law of trusts (Miles, this volume). If there are children, then an application under the Children Act 1989 is possible, however it has been suggested that Schedule 1 remains underutilized for the average income person as it has traditionally been used for big money cases (Mehta, 2015). The category of non-qualifying ceremony is reserved for those ceremonies which are so far removed from the requisite formalities that they fall outside the Marriage Act 1949 and are thus subject to no orders for financial relief. This can be particularly harsh in cases where

1 Prior to 2020, this category was described as a 'non-marriage' in case law, and that is reflected in the title of this chapter. However, following *Attorney General v Akhter and Khan* [2020] EWCA Civ 122, the term 'non-qualifying ceremony' was introduced, and therefore is used here.

the 'marriage' was of significant duration and produced children. The law does not specify the term 'non-qualifying ceremony'. Since the Marriage Act 1823, it has been the case that only a 'knowing and wilful' failure to comply with certain specified formalities will result in the finding of a void marriage (Probert, this volume). The wording of the 1823 Act sought to prevent any loopholes from being exploited by individuals hoping to evade their marriage obligations. At this point in time there were only three permitted entries to marriage, via the Anglican (Church of England) rites, Jewish or Quaker rites and of course, special provisions for the Royal Family.

The current Marriage Act 1949 sets out the formalities required to enter a marriage according to the rites of the Church of England or otherwise. Given the age of the current Act, it has been subject to a series of consolidating amendments, on a piecemeal basis; reactive in nature to cope with the stresses of the time. While it is not necessary to go through these amendments in any detail for present purposes, it is important to state that the Marriage Act 1949 allows for several routes into marriage. In particular, Part III of the Act sets out marriage in a register office, on 'approved premises' (hotels, restaurants and the like for civil ceremonies) and in a 'registered building' (for worship).

Despite these additions to the Marriage Act 1949, in British Muslim communities the uptake to register their places of worship has been low given that Muslims now number 3.37 million (ONS, 2018b). As of January 2018 there were only 395 Islamic religious buildings registered for the solemnization of marriage,[2] up from the 263 reported in 2015.[3] The inference from these figures is that for the majority of the group, most marriages must take place in a register

[2] HM Passport Office, 'Places of Worship Registered for Marriage', https://www.gov.uk/government/publications/places-of-worship-registered-for-marriage, accessed 16 January 2018.

[3] Hansard (6 July 2015) [HL], volume 764, column 88.

office. True Vision's survey of Muslim women found among their cohort of waves 2 and 3 that 88 per cent and 86 per cent respectively reported as having their marriage in a 'Registry [*sic*] Office/Town Hall' (True Vision, 2017). For British Muslims it is often necessary to 'marry twice', once in law and then again via the faith. Of itself, an Islamic marriage – the *nikah* – is not legally recognized under the Marriage Act 1949. It is this gap that can cause issues of validity and will be discussed later.

While it is simple to enter a lawful marriage, in terms of access to information and cost,[4] based on the lack of reported legal cases, it is possible to conclude that other comparable minority groups, Hindus and Sikhs being the most direct comparators, *do* comply and engage in lawful marriages, whether that be via Part III of the Marriage Act 1949, using a registered religious building as described previously, or by simply having both a religious ceremony in accordance with their beliefs and a civil ceremony in a register office or on approved premises. It remains a conundrum why British Muslims are falling short of completing the final step of registration.

But this failure of British Muslims to complete the legal marriage process does not seem to be a new issue. The community itself has been aware of this fact and it was one of the main reasons for the establishment of Sharia Councils in the mid-1980s (MLSCUK, 2018). This lack of compliance with marriage formalities has been an issue for a significant period of time now, and since the application of non-marriage/non-qualifying ceremony declarations, the harsh and unfair consequences have been really felt, to the detriment of British Muslim women. There are two types of Islamic marriages entered into by this diverse group: non-legally binding (religious only) marriages that are unrecognized by the law and those that are recognized. The former break down into

4 Information on marriage is widely published on all Council websites, and basic ceremonies start from £46.

two further groups, namely marriages being entered with or without informed consent.

Nikah marriage validity: case law guidance

In the case of *A-M v A-M (Divorce: Jurisdiction: Validity of Marriage)* the court commented that 'not every event to which somebody seeks to apply the label marriage' will fall within the statutory meaning.[5] There was concern about a floodgates argument regarding financial relief and an example was cited of a marriage ceremony conducted in a play or television programme, and how such events would be considered what are now termed non-qualifying ceremonies.[6] This is very sensible and begins to focus on the role of intention during the ceremony of marriage. However, the intention of the parties alone cannot convert a non-compliant marriage into a valid or void one.

In the case of *Dukali v Lamrani*[7] a British Moroccan couple both of the Muslim faith entered into what they both believed to be a legally binding ceremony of marriage. Their ceremony took place at the Moroccan consulate in Central London. They were together for around seven years and had one child. When the relationship broke down the wife filed for divorce, which prompted the husband to issue parallel divorce proceedings in Morocco. The divorce was granted in Morocco, with a very modest financial settlement being made for the wife. She applied to the English court, arguing that her right to apply for financial relief following an overseas divorce should be granted (Matrimonial and Family Proceedings Act 1984, Part III). The husband opposed the application for two reasons: first on the basis that there was no marriage capable

5 [2001] 2 FLR 6, at [63].

6 *Attorney General v Akhter and Khan* [2020] EWCA Civ 122.

7 [2012] EWHC 1748 (Fam).

of recognition under English law and second, on the basis that the Moroccan divorce should not be recognized under English law. The consulate marriage was found to be a non-marriage due to a lack of compliance with any of the requirements of the Marriage Act 1949.

While the dictum of the court in *A-M v A-M* remains sensible, English law generally fails to look beyond the form of ceremony when deciding marriage validity cases. The case of *Hudson v Leigh*[8] suggested that the following factors should be taken into account:

(a) whether the ceremony or event set out or purported to be a lawful marriage;
(b) whether it bore all or enough of the hallmarks of marriage;
(c) whether the three key participants believed, intended and understood the ceremony as giving rise to the status of lawful marriage;
(d) the reasonable perceptions, understandings and beliefs of those in attendance.

In later cases, however, judges have given more weight to the first two factors than to the intentions and perceptions of those involved. While the first two factors may appear objective, the analysis of whether a ceremony purported to be a lawful marriage and bore the hallmarks of a marriage will inevitably be filtered through cultural perceptions of what a marriage should look like. This presents a particular problem for British Muslims and other minority ethnic groups, whose ceremonies will be less familiar to the predominantly white male judiciary. Thus a ceremony may be classified as a non-qualifying ceremony even when the parties, witnesses and officiating official consider the ceremony to be effective. This can be seen most clearly in the case of *Dukali v Lamrani*. The difficult question remains as regards the difference between a non-, void and valid marriage.

[8] [2009] EWHC 1306 (Fam), at [77].

Cases avoiding non-qualifying ceremony

Recent cases concerning the issue of marriage validity have sought to clarify the law. The case of *MA v JA and the Attorney General*[9] avoided what was then termed non-marriage by recognizing that the *nikah* ceremony in question satisfactorily complied with sufficient of the statutory provisions. This was achieved on the basis that the ceremony took place within a registered building and that an authorized person was present.[10] The judge accepted that not all the requirements of the 1949 Act were complied with but that the ceremony was, in its character, the kind contemplated by the Act. As such there was an agreement between the parties and a marriage was created. Following the ceremony, the husband asked the Imam whether anything further was required of him but he was assured that they were married and nothing further needed to be done.

The first instance decision reached in the case of *Akhter v Khan*[11] continued with this flexible approach to marriage formalities, holding a knowingly unregistered Muslim marriage to be void. The judge was persuaded by an almost two-decade period of cohabitation, the presence of four children and the fact that the couple had resided in the UAE for a period of time as married. These factors prompted the court to consider Article 8 of the European Convention on Human Rights (ECHR) and approach section 11 of the Matrimonial Causes Act 1973 in a flexible manner, taking into account the best interests of the children. The court considered that for those couples who sought to effect or intended to effect a legally valid marriage, Article 8 of the ECHR 'supports an approach to interpretation and application [where] the finding of a decree of void marriage [is made] rather than a wholly invalid

9 [2012] EWHC 2219 (Fam).

10 Marriage Act 1949, ss 41 and 43.

11 [2018] EWFC 54.

marriage'.[12] It went on to say that given the circumstances of this particular case, as a public authority subject to Article 8, the court should avoid applying non-marriage as a term given its negative and potentially insulting connotations.

None of the requirements of the 1949 Act were complied with but the sentiment of the judge was made clear: 'the application of the term non-marriage to cases such as that before me feels instinctively inappropriate'.[13] The wife in this case asked repeatedly, over the course of the 18-year long relationship, for a civil marriage but the husband did not agree and thus their marriage was never formalized under English law.

This flexible approach seemed to demonstrate a turning point in the case law. However, upon appeal to the Court of Appeal, the first instance decision was set aside and the court found that there was 'no ceremony in respect of which a decree of nullity could be granted pursuant to the provisions of s.11'.[14]

Solutions to the Islamic marriage conundrum: understanding the context

My doctoral research conducted during 2012–13 focused on life histories of British Muslim women, shedding light on the wider socio-legal realties they faced upon the realization that their *nikah*-only marriages were not legally enforceable. All respondents reported that the traditional form (religiously valid) of marriage remains vitally important to them, their partner, and their respective families (Vora, 2016a). The 2017 Channel 4 documentary entitled *The Truth About Muslim Marriage* used a large-scale female-respondent survey and its results confirmed the knowledge of English marriage law and the importance of

12 [2018] EWFC 54, at [80].

13 [2018] EWFC 54, at [9].

14 [2020] EWCA Civ 122, at [128].

religious marriage and highlighted one reason for not having legally binding marriages (True Vision, 2017). Out of 897 respondents, 644 knew their marriage had no legal standing under English law[15] and of these, only 159 (out of a base line of 543) planned for a future civil wedding.

In these cases it seems that mandating a civil marriage as *The independent review into the application of sharia law in England and Wales* did (Home Office, 2018) creates an ultimatum; British Muslim couples need and want to comply with their traditions above all else. By creating a situation that mandates a civil marriage, the issue of choice is removed. Most British Muslims are aware of what they are doing, based on the Channel 4 survey and my own research. It does not appear to be a case of couples avoiding the law but rather testing their relationship before committing to a legally recognized relationship. Out of 500 respondents, 307 knew that completing a *nikah* alone did not mean that they were legally married under English law.[16] Conducting a *nikah* allows a young couple to enter marriage and enjoy its benefits. This is especially important for a community that still frowns upon open dating and having intimate relations outside of marriage. Out of 132 respondents, 46 delayed registration of their *nikah* marriage, citing reasons such as 'planning to register after a year or so' and 'wanted to make sure the marriage was going to work first'.[17]

From my doctoral study, one of my respondents, Jasmin, did not feel the need to formalize her marriage, it was a 'test-run' within the parameters of her religion, before making a legal

---

15 C4 survey question 22: 'Are you aware that without a legal civil ceremony performed by an official registrar in the UK, couples with a UK Nikah are not protected by the law the way that other married couples are?'

16 C4 survey (wave 2) question 7: 'Is it your understanding that your Nikah marriage alone means that you are legally married under British law?'

17 C4 survey (wave 3) question 11: 'If yes, why did or are you delaying your registration?'

commitment. This type of relationship has been referred to as halal dating (Mohee, 2011). Jasmin also went on to say that this is what the rest of society are doing by cohabiting rather than marrying (Vora, 2016a).

A striking observation to emerge from the Channel 4 survey data concerned the prevalence of non-legally binding Muslim marriages in Britain, a figure that has long been difficult to estimate. This difficulty has not stopped some from overestimating its incidence (Francois-Cerrah, 2015) without any methodologically sound evidence. Such statistics are not able to take into account the numbers of British Muslims marrying overseas (Gohir, 2015). In such overseas marriages, further registration is not required as private international law recognizes the *nikah* so long as it is deemed valid where celebrated. The most important survey finding was the 'without informed consent *nikah*-marriage', reported as between 17 and 28 per cent. *This* is the group that needs protection as it is these couples who believe, or intend, their marriage to be valid in law and thus enforceable. However, even with recent case law, it is difficult, expensive and complex to bring such a case to court. My research found that after the *nikah* ceremony was completed, there was little incentive for one party (usually the husband) to undertake a civil ceremony; he was able to enjoy the fruits of marriage without committing legally. I had several such case studies in my doctoral research and it was reported to me that it was impossible to compel the husband to go through the legal requirement of marriage. Women in such 'marriages' felt truly stuck whereas their 'husbands' were able to enjoy the benefits of married life without any of the financial burdens associated with its breakdown. This is most dangerous for women who do not hold assets, such as their house, car and business, in their own name. They are vulnerable and this vulnerability is exploited, more so when there are children involved. Asma Dukali's case demonstrated this danger very clearly; the family home was held in her husband's sole name and upon breakdown she was left with no financial remedy. The Moroccan divorce settlement made a very modest financial provision in her favour, though it would have cost more to visit Morocco to obtain it (Vora, 2016a). Nasreen Akhter's case also showed the same traits. As a qualified solicitor she understood the deficiency of her nuptial arrangement but was unable to compel her husband to follow through with a civil ceremony. Initially Nasreen 'won' her case in court though at the time of writing, her financial situation, following a very modest settlement, remains difficult. In comparison, her ex-husband still enjoys a good and comfortable quality of life.

When wives in such legally unrecognized relationships are unable to obtain recourse or remedy from the courts, they are left with no choice but to seek some kind of remedy from the Sharia Councils, who at the very least are able to provide them with a religious divorce and, in some cases, limited financial remedy. Enforcement of financial remedies is difficult as they also are not legally binding. Husbands pay one or two instalments and then stop (Vora, 2016b).

In the absence of case law to assist, what are the potential solutions?

What is needed is something that deters couples from entering into non-legally binding marriages, at least in their current form, which is without the informed consent of both parties. Providing both parties with clear guidance about their legal status should they not have a legally binding marriage ceremony in addition to their religiously validity marriage ceremony is essential. This is where the problem really lies: the gap between understanding what a *nikah*-only marriage means versus the protection a legally recognized ceremony of marriage brings. Furthermore, in my experience there appears to be an imbalance between the genders as regards this understanding (Vora 2016a).

Options could include fortification of cohabitation law. At present this fast-growing group are virtually unprotected. If there were some form of protection for cohabitees, then those parties in unrecognized Muslim marriages could be better protected. Such a mechanism does not require the cooperation of the other party but there are issues with this approach as there are fundamental differences between cohabitees and those who have undergone a ceremony of marriage, albeit a non-legal one.

I have previously proposed a classification model for cohabitation, seeking to give more accurate types of cohabiting couples, in line with the realities of present-day societal trends (Vora, 2016a). Currently all cohabiting relationships that are not civil partnerships or marriages are considered to fall under the single category of cohabitation. A single form of classification is crude as it fails to take into account the circumstances and background, factors such as the duration of the relationship, nature and extent of common residence, sexual relationships, property ownership, mutual commitment to a shared life, care and support of children, reputation and public aspects of the relationship. It seems unlikely that a young couple who have been cohabiting for 18 months are in the same position as an older couple with children who have been cohabiting for the previous 15 years. Furthermore, there are then those parties who may have married without completing all the formalities (including legal requirements) of marriage, who may not consider themselves cohabitees at all.

A tiered model of cohabitation allows for relationships to be better classified on the basis of circumstances and fact. I suggest that such a model would have three tiers: cohabitation, de facto and spousal:

(i) **Cohabitation** would be demarcated by a short-length relationship, a period of less than two years, with few (if any) shared assets, and no children.

(ii) **De facto** would entail those relationships subsisting for a period of at least two years, where the couple may have shared assets and have children and, on breakdown, similar factors as those for divorcing couples will apply when assessing the relevant financial orders applicable.

(iii) **Spousal** would be reserved for those who consider themselves as married because they have undergone a religiously valid ceremony of marriage without completing the legal requirements. Under these circumstances no duration requirement would be applicable.

The reasoning for these tiers is transparent; they take into account the decision of the parties in (i) and (ii) who have chosen not to marry. In terms of providing financial benefit, in particular to those who fall under tier (ii), the model does not seek to treat them as if they actually had married but seeks to relieve the unequal impact of the relationship based on children. Likewise for those falling under tier (iii), there exists no prescribed duration of relationship as the couple have chosen to get married by virtue of their religiously valid marriage ceremony.

Location of marriage ceremonies

As a second option, the gap between *nikah* and civil marriage is fundamental as post–*nikah* it can be difficult to engage in a civil ceremony of marriage. The current law requires marriages to take place in a prescribed place before a particular person. Could the establishment of a celebrant-based system of marriage both update marriage law and solve this issue? It would be the celebrant who was responsible for complying with the formalities of marriage, thereby providing the couple with a professional and efficient service. Couples would be at liberty to get married wherever they wanted, including private homes. The institution of marriage would be protected because a professional person would be responsible, in law, for ensuring that the rules were abided by. But more importantly couples would be engaging in a form of marriage that really meant something to them and there would be no gap. Indeed, such a system operates in Scotland and at the time of writing there have been no reported cases of unregistered Muslim marriages (Vora, 2016b).

Conclusion

The issue of unrecognized Muslim marriage is a niche problem and assessing relationships based on the factual matrix seems a sensible way of finding a solution, and where necessary and possible, avoiding a declaration of non-qualifying ceremony Post–*nikah* there is little, if anything, one party can do to compel their partner to undergo a civil ceremony. Any solution has to consider this point. While the first instance decision in *Akhter v Khan* suggested a slight shift in case law, being the second example of the court taking a flexible approach to avoid the harsh realities of non-qualifying ceremonies this was rejected on appeal, confirming the position that case law alone cannot solve the issue. As outlined previously, this must be done either through some form of cohabitation classification or by altering the current requirements of the Marriage Act 1949, allowing couples to marry in a way that is meaningful to them and removing the requirement of place, thus preventing the occurrence of uninformed unregistered marriages.

With 3.4 million cohabiting couples in England and Wales (ONS, 2019) and the common law marriage myth well entrenched in society (Barlow, this volume), this topic does not exclusively concern British Muslims. A solution based on firm legal foundations that takes into account these families is required.

The law concerning non-qualifying ceremonies might change via a decision of the Supreme Court, or a full re-write of the Marriage Act 1949. In late 2018 the Treasury announced that 'the Government will ask the Law Commission to review the laws around weddings in England and Wales … [and] the project will look to propose options for a simpler and fairer system to give modern couples meaningful choice' (Law Commission, 2018). This project is under way at the time of writing and much rides upon its highly anticipated outcome.

SIX

Religious-Only Marriages and Cohabitation: Deciphering Differences

Rajnaara C. Akhtar

Introduction

The independent review into the application of sharia law in England and Wales (Home Office, 2018) focussed on the implementation of 'Sharia law' by Sharia Councils. It proposed reforms to tackle the use of Sharia Councils, including legislative changes aimed at reducing the incidence of religious-only non-civilly registered marriages. The review has faced criticism on a number of issues. The key argument of this chapter is that any legal reform to address the negative outcomes of religious-only marriages should not be targeted solely at these relationships, but should rather encompass all cohabiting couples, who currently have very limited protection under the family law regime. The central premise of this argument is that the lack of rights for all cohabiting couples has been a long-standing failing of family law in England and Wales (Barlow et al, 2005). Religious-only marriages may be conceptually different from cohabitation, but the legal consequences remain the same. Therefore, the negative outcomes of both relationship types are very similar for the most vulnerable party – almost invariably the woman – making differing legal treatment unwarranted.

The *Independent review* was additionally concerned with potential discrimination against Muslim women using Sharia Councils (Home Office, 2018: 3), of which many are in non-legally recognized marriages. However, as research demonstrates that women in all informal relationships bear great risk, including far larger numbers of cohabitees, law reform must cohesively respond to the needs of all such women rather than singling out any particular group. This chapter therefore argues that any law reform must be more generic and cover all families within informal cohabiting relationships. While Muslim couples may not view themselves as cohabitants, the law will treat them as such and in England and Wales, this means very limited family law protections are available (Miles, this volume). While religious-only Muslim weddings in many cases may be celebrated with pomp and ceremony, the lack of legal recognition means these become 'marriages in another form' and not 'cohabitation by another name'. However, these underlying differences should not dictate law reform proposals, and the focus should instead be on the negative legal outcomes experienced by those within all such legally unrecognized relationships.

Independent review recommendations

The *Independent review* recommendations were threefold. First, it recommended amendments to the Marriage Act 1949 and the Matrimonial Causes Act 1973, purportedly to 'unify' Islamic marriages in line with 'Christian' and Jewish marriages; secondly, it advocated an awareness campaign on the legal consequences of religious-only marriages; and finally, it recommended regulation of Sharia Councils (Home Office, 2018: 5–6). The issue of religious-only marriages is presented as being a particular problem because of the risk that a marriage recognized as such within the parties' own community, if not by the law, will break down, leaving the woman homeless and penniless. This 'paradigm case of unregistered marriages'

(Akhtar 2018c: 146), while clearly an issue, oversimplifies the way in which Muslim marriage practices are evolving both in England and Wales, and other similar countries around the world where Muslims are a minority.

The first of the proposals was for Muslim couples to be required to enter a civil marriage at the same time as, or preceding, the Islamic marriage. To reinforce this, it called for amendments to sections 75 to 77 of the Marriage Act 1949, which deal with the offences that may be committed by those involved in solemnizing and registering marriages. These proposed amendments would criminalize celebrants unless they ensured that the religious ceremony of marriage they conducted would be legally recognized or that a civil ceremony had already taken place. Of course, a *nikah* can be performed in the absence of an imam, meaning this can easily be circumvented, however, it is usual practice within British Muslim communities to have an imam or equivalent present.

These proposed amendments to the law, the *Independent review* argues, would reduce the rate of occurrence of religious-only marriages. However, the first proposal also means that individual autonomy is overridden by the state, especially as far as those Muslims *choosing* to be in an informal unregistered religious-only marriage are concerned. While for the latter couple an imam may not be necessary as any person or the couple themselves (with or without a guardian for the woman) can perform the marriage, the proposed legal changes mean such an option becomes illegitimate at best and bordering on illegality at worst. This recommendation could result in a move towards policing Muslim relationships, which should be cautioned against in the strongest possible terms.

The *Independent review*'s approach is clearly inconsistent with the 'new respect' (Sandberg and Thompson, 2016: 190) for individual autonomy seen in family law in England and Wales and in particular to the approach taken in legal proceedings on the family. The problematization of Muslim marriages (Moors, 2018) is responsible for the development of an interventionist narrative, which would result in the autonomy of one particular faith group being significantly constrained. Informal marriage practices need to be understood in the context of Muslim relationship norms, which are still built around notions of religiosity and sanctity in the eyes of God. For observant Muslims, access to informal marriage and sexual freedom are interdependent. A religious-only marriage is a way of simultaneously navigating Muslim religious norms and European cultural norms relating to the formation of relationships. It can facilitate 'dating', enabling a couple to get to know each other, or cohabitation, allowing them to test their relationship. It may also precede an engagement period during which the couple are planning their (legally recognized) wedding. The crucial point to note here is that any restriction on the performance of a religious-only marriage is also a restriction on individual sexual freedom, as observant Muslims will not enter such relationships without the *nikah* being performed. However, entering a religious marriage does not necessarily mean the couple are ready to enter a legally recognized one. As a result, any restriction on flexibility in the use of the *nikah* for these purposes is an unfair and unacceptable restriction on individual liberty. Due to this complexity, the solution does not lie in tackling this particular relationship type, but rather in addressing the increasing numbers of couples in general who are in non-legally recognized relationships and who are left without legal protection. This would include those in religious-only marriages who live together and therefore offset the paradigm case.

The contrast between these proposals and the treatment of cohabitees in England and Wales could not be starker. For the latter group, individual autonomy is safeguarded despite a plethora of case law reflecting decades of struggle faced by these couples. Cohabitation, like religious-only marriages, can have a number of underlying motives. Similarly, many cohabiting couples still labour under the false impression of 'common law' rights arising from their relationship despite this having no legal significance (Barlow, this volume). While the two relationship types may be conceptually different, the legal outcomes are the same and therefore the legal treatment must be consistent. Calls for legal rights for cohabitants have been made for some time, with the Cohabitation Rights Bill – a Private Member's Bill – being regularly introduced into Parliament.

Despite these shortcomings, one aspect of the *Independent review*'s recommendations is to be welcomed. There is a clear need for an awareness campaign as the complexity of the varied reasons for remaining 'unregistered' revealed through research suggests that many fail to either understand the significance of going through a legally binding ceremony, or do not give primacy to it (Akhtar, 2015). Couples are either not taking advantage of the possibility of marrying in a registered religious building or, if planning to have two separate ceremonies, are not prioritizing the civil ceremony while the larger religious wedding celebrations are being planned. Any change in culture here will require a concerted effort to change the narrative, which an awareness campaign is well placed to achieve.

Why religious-only?

The motivations for entering a religious-only marriage are not uniform and depend very much on the individual circumstances of the couple. While case law such as *Akhter v Khan*[1] speaks to marriages which are long established and where one party is denying the other a formal legally recognized marriage, the landscape is often far more complex and reflective of many interwoven factors. However, it should be noted that the *Independent review* and much political intervention is based primarily on the disadvantages faced by women in the *Akhter v Khan* scenario. While this is undoubtedly an important issue

1 [2018] EWFC 54; *Attorney General v Akhtar and Khan* [2020] EWCA Civ 122.

requiring legal resolution, the lens through which solutions are proposed must be much wider and cognizant of the range of underlying reasons for religious-only marriages occurring.

My previous research in this area has demonstrated that couples do not prioritize the civil ceremony where religious wedding celebrations are being planned (Akhtar, 2015: 153). The relatively small number of mosques registered for marriage also limits the availability of religious ceremonies being conducted in a form that attracts legal recognition (Vora, this volume). The *nikah* is viewed as being the key part of marriage and therefore it represents the essential component which will always form the central pillar of Muslim marriage rites. It should be noted that being cognizant of this when proposing legal reforms to marriage laws means acknowledging the form of ceremony which will definitely take place, and proposing reform which either takes account of this, or simplifies legal processes to enable both to occur at the same time in a greater number of potential settings.

More significantly, there has been a particular cultural shift among young Muslims and their relationship norms, which is being revealed in research findings. Young people in general are more cautious about making marital commitments early, however, those youth who are religiously observant will not enter an intimate relationship without a religious marriage in place. Young Muslims appear to be adapting new relationship norms as they navigate religious laws, community norms, wider peer group behaviours, and the law. Of course, 'young Muslims' are not a homogeneous group, however a survey conducted in 2016 found that they are the most likely group to be in religious-only marriages, with 80 per cent of respondents below the age of 24 and married stating they were 'unregistered' (True Vision, 2017). Narratives around marriage are also shifting in this group, and issues such as 'choice', 'independent decision', 'informed decisions' and not being 'forced' to marry formally all form part of the discourse (Akhtar 2018a: 438).

It is clear that as younger generations of Muslims are responding to their contexts, relationship behaviour is beginning to mirror wider peer group cultural norms, though carefully constructed around religious principles. Therefore, young couples may use religious-only marriages to test their relationships before committing fully. They may also want to begin those relationships earlier and thus their marriages may look like dating, an engagement or cohabitation to those outside the Muslim community. Removing the choice of informal marriages for these couples raises the potential for early or premature formal marriages, which could result in negative consequences for couples not yet ready for that commitment, either emotionally, financially or on other relevant fronts. It would also remove their ability to test their relationships before legally committing to each other, and their freedom to be in intimate relationships without involving the state. This raises serious questions for a liberal democracy which has obligations to respect human rights, including those stipulated in the European Convention on Human Rights (ECHR) such as freedom of religion (Article 9), the right to marry (Article 12) and right to private family life (Article 8). The relationship behaviour of young Muslims is highly significant as the 2011 census revealed that 50 per cent of the Muslim population was under the age of 25, with 33 per cent aged below 15, compared with 17.6 per cent for the population as a whole (Muslim Council of Britain Report, 2015). These statistics clearly demonstrate that young Muslims cannot be disregarded where law reform impacting on Muslim marriages is being proposed.

Other legal incentives may be driving changes in relationship behaviour. For example, transnational relationships in Muslim communities are in decline, and therefore the need for state recognition of the marriage for immigration purposes is no longer a factor for many couples (Muslim Marriage Working Group, 2012). While this may have accounted for a larger number of legally recognized marriages in the past, it is no longer a motivating factor. On the other hand, still focussed on migration, where refugees are concerned, they may face difficulties in accessing a legally recognized marriage due to a lack of documentation (Akhtar, 2018b). For these individuals, a religious-only marriage may be the only option, at least temporarily.

Lack of registration may not always be a conscious decision, however. For some couples, the marriage norms in their countries of origin may lead to confusion regarding legal obligations in the UK. Here, one or both individuals may falsely believe the *nikah* performed by the imam is recognized by the state, in line with practices in their countries of origin. Such confusion can be overcome by placing an obligation on any individual performing religious marriages to inform the parties of the legal status of their religious marriage. Such an obligation is less onerous than the proposed criminalization of imams.

Criminalizing imams?

One particularly unhelpful suggestion in the *Independent review* was the idea of criminalizing imams for performing religious-only marriages. Amendments were proposed to sections 75 to 77 of the Marriage Act 1949 to achieve this. Given that couples can enter into a *nikah* without an imam being present, such reforms would potentially have only a limited effect on the number of religious-only marriages. As mentioned previously, it would, however, create a climate of intolerance of such marriages and amount to policing of Muslim relationships, with a restriction on who can perform a religious marriage. Imams also play a central role in the spiritual and family lives of Muslims, being one of the first ports of call in family disputes for many (Akhtar, 2019). Criminalizing imams in this way may undermine their wider roles within Muslim communities, especially their role as spiritual guides.

Imams perform the majority of religious marriages,[2] however these can potentially occur in a range of venues. The True Vision Survey found that only 31 per cent of marriages surveyed were performed in a mosque, with a further 31 per cent being performed at the wedding venue and 38 per cent being performed at home. Current legislation already regulates marriages performed by authorized persons from any of the faith groups in buildings registered for solemnizing marriages. However, it should be noted that of the three venues identified – the mosque, wedding venue, and home – only a mosque and potentially some 'other' wedding venues could be covered by existing legislation. A marriage performed at home, or in a restaurant or other similar non-registered venue, will not be, demonstrating the limitations in the current law. Under section 75(2), where a couple have complied with the Marriage Act and given notice, any imam who 'knowingly and wilfully' solemnizes a marriage anywhere other than the registered building for marriage is already committing an offence. Thus, the *Independent review* in fact seeks to introduce major law reform (Probert, 2018b), whereby no imam can perform any religious marriage, at any venue, unless that marriage is itself in accordance with the law or has been preceded by a civil ceremony. This is in stark contrast to the *Independent review*'s claim to simply be advocating a change in the law to bring the law applicable to Islamic marriages in line with the law relating to other religious marriages.

As set out previously, a significant concern here is that such drastic steps would no doubt lead to a climate of intolerance towards religious-only marriages, even for couples who *choose* this form of marriage, and the policing of Muslim relationships. There are potentially serious consequences for young Muslim couples in particular, who are most likely to be in unregistered

[2] 81 per cent in Mosques, 69 per cent at home, 73 per cent in wedding halls (True Vision, 2017).

marriages. This can no doubt lead to further alienation in an already hostile political and security environment.

Deciphering differences

Just as couples entering religious-only marriages have a range of motivations, so do cohabitees. These include 'a prelude to marriage', 'do it yourself' marriage, or a rejection of legal marriage (Barlow et al, 2008: 65, 68, 72). Barlow et al's (2005) earlier study also identified reasons for couples choosing to cohabit, such as wanting to avoid stereotyped gender roles which are associated with marriage, a disillusionment with the very idea of marriage, wanting to avoid divorce should things go wrong, wanting the emotional security provided by living together, or other compelling reasons such as an unexpected pregnancy. Finally, the cost of a 'proper' wedding was a significant factor.

Where misconceptions about legal rights are concerned, Barlow's research shows the percentage of respondents believing that cohabitants either 'definitely' or 'probably' have the same rights as married people fell from over to just under half between 2000 and 2019 (Barlow, this volume). However, a 2017 study by Resolution found that a higher percentage of two thirds of cohabitees were unaware that there was no such thing as a 'common law marriage' in legal terms,[3] suggesting that despite work to increase awareness, the situation has not improved. Just as with religious-only marriages, the myth of the common law marriage can give rise to a false sense of security for families.

So what are the differences between a religious-only marriage and cohabitation? Conceptually, these relationships

---

3 'Millions of couples at severe financial risk due to "common-law marriage myth"', 27 November 2017, https://resolution.org.uk/news/millions-of-couples-at-severe-financial-risk-due-to-common-law-marriage-myth/ (accessed 28 August 2019).

are very different as Muslim couples are unlikely to call themselves cohabitees. Indeed, in the first instance decision in *Akhter v Khan*, Williams J referred to the ECHR Article 8 right to private family life, and did in fact differentiate between simple cohabitation and certain types of religious-only marriages, stating:

> It does not seem to me that there is a distinction in Article 8 terms between those who cohabit choosing not to marry and those who knowingly undertake a religious only ceremony and opt not to undertake the additional formalities necessary to affect [*sic*] a valid legal marriage. However I do consider that in respect of those who sought to effect or intended to effect a legal marriage that article 8 supports an approach to interpretation and application which the finding of a decree of a void marriage rather than a wholly invalid marriage.[4]

Despite failing to comply with the requirements of a legally valid marriage, the marriage in *Akhter v Khan* was held at first instance to be void under the Matrimonial Causes Act 1973 (MCA) rather than a non-marriage. A 'flexible approach' was incorporated in applying section 11 of the MCA, taking into account Articles 8 and 12 ECHR and the best interests of children. In this case, human rights principles were used to declare a religious-only marriage arising from a *nikah* to be a void marriage for the purposes of the Act. This crucially would give rise to financial relief applications, which a declaration of non-qualifying ceremony does not. The further reliance on the horizontal impact of Article 12 by women whose husbands withhold a legally binding marriage was an interesting proposal. Here, Williams J stated that the husband himself is obstructing the wife's right to marry.[5] However, arguments

[4] *Akhter v Khan* [2018] EWFC 54, at [80].

[5] *Akhter v Khan* [2018], at [83].

about the applicability of Article 1 Protocol 1 rights to 'peaceful enjoyment of possessions' were rejected, preventing any broader claims on presumed shared assets. The first instance decision was set aside on appeal,[6] and reasoning based on Articles 8 and 12 was rejected.

While it is easy to argue that the conceptual differences between cohabitation and a religious-only marriage are of no significance to the state, the first instance decision in this case demonstrated a *potential* differing outcome for those couples who *intended* or *sought* a legal marriage. However, the Court of Appeal took the position that 'mere intention cannot change the legal effect of a ceremony of marriage'.[7] In any event, on the facts of the case, Mr Khan did not actually intend a legal marriage despite leading Ms Akhter to believe otherwise. Thus, despite a professed intention or expectation to enter into a legally recognized ceremony, the outcome will still be a non-qualifying ceremony.

This position is challenged by couples who self-identify as being married following a marriage ceremony and quite often the ceremony of marriage and accompanying celebrations will involve a similar public display of commitment to that involved in a legally valid wedding. These weddings bear all the hallmarks of traditional ceremonies, usually being evidenced by a written *nikah* contract. Cohabitants, on the other hand, tend not to undergo any form of ceremony and usually do not present themselves as being married (although arguably some might). The first instance approach in *Akhter v Khan*, where the marriage was only deemed void if coupled with the requisite intention to formally marry, seems logical in the absence of family rights for cohabitants. In practical terms, however, the appeal decision reinforced the tenuousness of this position and the need for couples to engage with the formal legal processes in some way. Further, pursuing such recognition of a religious

6 [2020] EWCA Civ 122.

7 [2020] EWCA Civ 122, at [97].

marriage requires access to resources to enable the matter to be tested in court. This is similar to the burden of weight on cohabitees establishing legal rights, usually through property law or equity principles. This is not an adequate long-term solution. Law reform must enable easier access to property and financial provision for all couples who live together as a family. The idea of 'couple regulation' (Barlow and James 2004: 148), which seeks to protect the function rather than the form of relationships, is particularly persuasive.

Beyond the intent and ceremonial aspects outlined previously, the question arises as to why the *Independent review* and those calling for targeted law reform to tackle Muslim marriages believe that Muslim women need greater protection than other cohabitees. Even in a situation where religious-only marriages are occurring in 60 per cent of cases, the women impacted clearly will not fall within a homogeneous category. The cases coming to court and covered in the media are of relatively higher net worth couples,[8] thus involving mainly Muslim middle class families. It is likely that the majority of Muslim couples will not fall within a high net worth category (Muslim Council of Britain Report, 2015: 58–61). Further to this, factors such as economic activity, wealth and children all impact upon financial resolution. For example, the presence of children is clearly an aggravating factor where poor financial outcomes for women are concerned. However, statistics show that *all* women are impacted on by having children (Fawcett Society, 2010) as they tend to begin part-time work and

[8] For example, the battle over a property worth £2.2 million reported in the *Manchester Evening News*. 'Why this £2m mansion a Man United player wanted to buy is at the centre of a courtroom battle', 7 April 2019, https://www.manchestereveningnews.co.uk/news/greater-manchester-news/2m-mansion-man-united-player-16067576?fbclid=IwAR1UpR9jqXqAPB05ZuOhHB3lVBKRyKsYmgXGy-bYUJF0E9jeNjgQ-j_g8Aw (accessed 28 August 2019).

become less financially secure (ONS, 2019). Mothers with children aged between one and 11 years are more likely to be in part-time employment than full-time employment, with only a quarter of women with a child aged one being in full-time employment. Thus, the impact of the breakdown of a religious-only marriage can be expected to be greater for women with children, where no financial remedies are available other than basic maintenance for children under Schedule 1 of the Children Act. However, this outcome would also be the same for any cohabiting mother, negating the need for special treatment for the former. Further, if there are no assets between the couple, financial resolution becomes pointless and therefore for such couples in religious-only marriages, a long-winded divorce is not helpful.

Nevertheless, the argument that the 'existence of a law of non-marriage and the resulting inability to make a financial claim is indirectly discriminatory in respect both of women and in particular Muslim women'[9] is hard to disagree with. As Williams J pointed out, both are 'disproportionately affected given the likelihood that men will usually hold the majority of financial assets and Muslim women are more likely to be held to be in a non-marriage given the current state of the law'.[10] However, one solution for all such vulnerable women is still a fairer solution.

'Knowingly and willingly'

In a development of the flexible approach to section 11 MCA seen in the first instance decision in *Akhter v Khan*, in the absence of rights for cohabitants, perhaps it is time to go one step further. A point of departure between a cohabiting relationship and an informal religious-only marriage could be knowledge,

9 *Akhter v Khan* [2018] EWFC 54, at [75].

10 *Akhter v Khan*, at [75].

intent or belief. Where one or both parties believed their Islamic marriage ceremony had legal effect, there should be some form of correlating recognition. Here, there would be no intent not to comply with marriage formalities, but rather a complete lack of knowledge that those formalities were required. There was intent to marry however, which could be evidenced by the ceremony of marriage itself. A state which requires marriage formalities to be adhered to should afford some recognition to those who genuinely intended to marry. On this ground, cohabitants can be distinguished as such couples have no similar intent. This would serve to uphold the institution of marriage, while taking a lenient approach to those who have failed to engage the requisite state infrastructure. However, one obvious difficulty would be the unlikelihood that both parties would make the same argument, especially where it results in financial compromise for the wealthier spouse. Thus, it would fall upon the spouse seeking legal recognition to prove that the belief was jointly held. However, this reasoning could also be extended to cohabitees who believe in the common law marriage myth. Therefore, the argument for relief for all non-legally recognized families still holds sway.

Conclusion

While it is clear that some of those in religious-only marriages do need legal protection, it would be deeply objectionable to limit the autonomy of all Muslims to form relationships as they wish in order to achieve this. Relationships come in all forms, shapes and sizes in the UK today. The particular problematization of Muslim marriages is unhelpful, as cohabitees have faced the same legal outcomes to their relationships for decades, despite similar confusion over their rights. One legal solution which covers both relationship types will help to overcome the issue in a more comprehensive way, without any particular community being isolated for targeted reform.

Young Muslims and their evolving relationship behaviours need particular attention as the most significant evidence of non-legally recognized marriages is found in those under 24 years of age. Ironically, this cultural shift in relationship behaviour of British Muslims can be seen as a sign of integration rather than separation.

At the time of writing, the rejection on appeal of the first instance decision in *Akhter v Khan* reinforces religious-only marriages being classified as non-qualifying ceremonies, even in the instance where one party's desire for a civil registration and expectation of a civil registration are prevented by a reluctant spouse. Those who falsely believed they were protected by the law while remaining unregistered, and who lack the resources to legally challenge an assumption of a non-qualifying ceremony status, require a different legal solution. Family rights for cohabitees are long overdue, and the issue of religious-only marriages may well provide the political impetus to resolve the issues, if for all the wrong reasons!

SEVEN

From Regulating Marriage Ceremonies to Recognizing Marriage Ceremonies

Rehana Parveen

Introduction

English law has developed a complex set of rules and regulations to determine what types of marriage ceremonies create the legal status of 'marriage'. Failures to fulfil these legal requirements have led to confusing outcomes as courts grapple with the consequences of non-compliance. The current rules and regulations do not reflect the diverse ways in which members of Britain's multi-cultural, multi-ethnic, multi-religious and non-religious society enters into marriages. Muslims in particular have been highlighted as a community who are increasingly undertaking marriage ceremonies that do not comply with the requirements of English law, resulting in Muslim couples being held to be parties to what is now termed a 'non-qualifying ceremony'.[1] It is proposed that Muslims themselves should be able to determine when and how they marry and the state's interest is protected by a post-ceremony registration system, not unlike the registration of a birth or death. A liberal state

1 Following *Attorney General v Akhter and Khan* [2020] EWCA Civ 122.

should not be regulating the ceremonial aspects of a marriage; rather its interest lies in recognizing a marriage and providing protection to its citizens against harm or other vulnerabilities. Such protection can be achieved without the policing of the marriage ceremony itself.

The 'Muslim problem'

It has become increasingly recognized that within a diverse, multi-ethnic, multi-religious and multi-cultural society, members of that society will wish to enter into marriage ceremonies that reflect the cultural, religious and social habits of the communities with which they associate and interact (Law Commission, 2015). For most people, though not all, a marriage ceremony is a public proclamation of their relationship and individuals may wish to make this proclamation in a manner which is meaningful to them. English law has historically concentrated its energies on establishing formalities in order to regulate the steps up to and including the ceremony itself as a method for determining which marriages are granted the status of a legally recognized marriage. English law requires the parties to have taken specific steps prior to the marriage ceremony from which it can be ensured that they, *among other things*, were above minimum age requirements, not already validly married and not otherwise precluded from marrying each other.[2]

In focussing on the policing of the ceremony itself, English law has, perhaps understandably, aligned itself with a Christian ceremony of marriage as the benchmark from which to judge whether a particular ceremony amounts to a legally recognized marriage (see Vora, this volume). Successive Marriage Acts have been modelled with Christian denominations in mind, which has inevitably resulted in rigidity in the law, thus making it

---

[2] Matrimonial Causes Act 1973, s 11.

more difficult for an alternative ceremony or set of rites to be recognized as a valid ceremony capable of conferring the legal status of marriage. The formality rules have been criticized as being unnecessarily complex, leading to confusing outcomes where there have been breaches (Gaffney-Rhys, 2010, 2013; Le Grice, 2013; Probert, 2002, 2013; Vora, 2016b; O'Sullivan and Jackson, 2017; Probert and Barton, 2018; Probert and Saleem, 2018). Breaches of the formality requirements can lead to a marriage being declared void,[3] what is now termed a 'non-qualifying ceremony',[4] or, depending on the nature of the breach and the mental state of the parties, valid.[5] Much of the recent case law around 'non-qualifying ceremonies' has concerned Muslim marriage ceremonies where none or very few of the formalities of English law have been observed. This, coupled with academic research and media reports, suggests that we are seeing a specific trend emerging among Muslims in failing to fulfil the requirements of English law (True Vision, 2017; Home Office, 2018: 17). Traditionally Muslims would meet the requirements of English law by undertaking a separate civil ceremony in addition to the religious one, in effect getting married twice (Pearl and Menski, 1988). What some Muslims appear to be doing now is to get married only once, and that once is by virtue of the religious ceremony (Akhtar, 2015; Vora, 2016b; Parveen, 2018b).

The narrative around Muslim marriage practices has been to present them as uniquely challenging in this context. In *The independent review into the application of sharia law in England and Wales* (Home Office, 2018), little attempt was made to situate Muslim practices in forming intimate relationships

---

3 *Akhter v Khan* [2018] EWFC 54.

4 *Attorney General v Akhter and Khan* [2020] EWCA Civ 122. Formerly termed a 'non-marriage': *Shagroon v Sharbatly* [2012] EWCA Civ 1507; *Dukali Lamrani* [2012] EWHC 1748 (Fam); *El Gamal v Al-Maktoum* [2011] EWCH 3763 (Fam).

5 *MA v JA and the Attorney General* [2012] EWHC 2219 (Fam).

within the wider context of British society and the manner in which non-Muslims are entering into formally or informally recognized relationships. There are two problematic aspects to this narrative. The first is the notion that Muslim marriage ceremonies or Muslim marriage practices more generally are so different from any other marriage practices that their accommodation within English law is almost impossible. The second is the assumption that the failure of Muslims to enter into recognized marriages is indicative of a lack of integration within British society (Casey Review, 2016). As a consequence, the state's response is likely to be targeted explicitly towards Muslims only and, at best, aimed at encouraging Muslims to marry in the manner in which the state currently requires. At worst, the state will introduce legislation compelling Muslims to enter into legally recognized marriages with the threat of criminal sanctions if they fail to do so (Home Office, 2018).[6] In either case these are very narrow and unimaginative solutions which fail to pay attention to wider developments in family law.

In the next section this narrative is explored in more detail and some of the complexities it raises are highlighted.

Framing this topic and the complex issues to navigate

It is clear that there is an emerging trend whereby some Muslims are entering into *nikah*-only marriages (Shah-Kazemi, 2001; Bano, 2004, Douglas et al, 2012). However, it is far from clear how widespread this trend is or, more importantly, why Muslims might be choosing this route. Most of the academic research has examined *nikah*-only marriages within the context of relationships that have broken down, very often as part of an exploration of the role of *shari'a* councils. Additionally, much of the qualitative data has come only from women. While their

6 See also the 'Register Our Marriage' campaign.

experiences provide an important source of data, the research to date offers a very specific and narrow lens.

The overall picture is incomplete if there is little information from unmarried Muslims contemplating future relationships, or from those who are happily 'married' about the type of marriage that they are in and why, or more specifically from Muslim men. Research specifically aimed at investigating *nikah*-only marriages more broadly is beginning to emerge (Akhtar, 2015, 2018a, 2018b, 2018c; Vora, 2016b; Uddin, 2018). In my own research, a particularly revealing category, although very small, was that of Muslim women who had undergone both a civil and Islamic divorce. The women's reflections on how their experiences of the civil system may impact on their choices for future marriage arrangements were perhaps surprising. One would expect this category to be the most informed as to the benefits of a civil marriage, and yet there was overwhelming support for *nikah*-only marriages in any future relationship arrangements (Parveen, 2017, 2018b). This is supported by Uddin's separate study, in which he also identified Muslim women who had previously been divorced via the civil courts subsequently choosing to enter into *nikah*-only marriages (Uddin, 2018).

In exploring whether Muslim marriage arrangements present a unique challenge to English law Nash draws together the evidence which supports the ease with which a *nikah* may be entered into (Nash, 2017). In contrast to the formalities of English law, a *nikah* does not require a registered building, nor does it require an authorized person to register the ceremony (Ali, 2008; Tucker, 2008; Black et al, 2013; Edge, 2013). Indeed, many of the formalities laid down by English law either before or at the time of the ceremony are irrelevant to the validity of a *nikah* (Parveen, 2017). This, coupled with the notion that for most Muslims it would seem that they consider themselves 'married' by the *nikah*, indicates that Muslims are sufficiently satisfied as to the legitimacy of their relationships without necessarily obtaining state approval (Bano, 2004;

Akhtar, 2015; Vora, 2016b; Parveen, 2018b; Uddin, 2018).[7] The ease of the *nikah* ceremony does present challenges to English law should it wish to accommodate the actual *nikah* ceremony into its current framework (Edge, 2013; Nash, 2017; Parveen, 2017).

If, as the current body of research seems to indicate, the *nikah* ceremony provides Muslims with legitimacy and they, in effect, attribute to themselves the status of marriage, at least among their own social and familial circles, then the question to ask is: why would Muslims undertake the additional formalities to obtain state recognition? Muslim marriage practices must be understood within the wider British context of increasing cohabitation among non-Muslims,[8] a greater focus on autonomy and choice, increasing privatization of family dispute resolution (Diduck, 2016) and a greater recognition of rights within the family unconnected to a legally recognized marriage (see Miles, this volume). Akhtar argues that contextualizing Muslim family practices within wider social norms indicates that religious-only marriages are signs of cultural transitions for Muslims and of 'integration' rather than 'isolation' (Akhtar, 2018a). If state recognition of a relationship is unimportant to many British non-Muslims who cohabit rather than enter into a state-sanctioned marriage, and English law itself is slowly establishing rights and duties unconnected to marital status, why would a legally recognized marriage be any more important to Muslims?

Nikah-only marriages that have been declared either non-marriages or void marriages occupy a particularly anomalous

7 There has been no academic research which has indicated Muslims do *not* consider themselves married despite having entered into a *nikah*. Overwhelmingly the research supports the notion that Muslims consider themselves to be 'married' or at the very least in a relationship that has religious, cultural and familial legitimacy, irrespective of any state recognition.

8 ONS (2019).

position. The research tells us that these marriage ceremonies are recognized as legitimate by the couples who enter into them and by the communities in which they participate (Shah-Kazemi, 2001; Bano, 2004, 2012; Akhtar, 2015, 2018a, 2018c; Parveen, 2018b; Uddin, 2018). The couples expect to undergo a religiously sanctioned process for the termination of their relationships, whether by the husband pronouncing a *talaq*, or the wife accessing a *shari'a* council, or some other method. This is all irrespective of whether the state recognizes these relationships.

While the law has not to date recognized *nikah*-only marriages as valid, even this cannot be said with absolute certainty as case law continues to evolve.[9] The answer to the question of why Muslims may be entering into *nikah*-only marriages without the protection of a civil marriage is as least as complex, if not more complex, than asking why non-Muslims are cohabiting rather than marrying. There are multiple motivations (Akhtar, 2015, 2018c; Uddin, 2018) and for many couples, whether Muslim or not, this issue only becomes important at the time of dissolution. The multiple motivations of Muslims have not yet been fully explored. From the limited research that we have, we do know that for some Muslims it is a choice not to be bound by state regulation, for others it is a lack of knowledge as to the requirements of state law (Shah-Kazemi, 2001; Bano, 2004, 2012; Akhtar, 2015; Parveen, 2017; Uddin, 2018). For many it seems the civil ceremony does not have sufficient priority to warrant the additional time and effort needed to organize it and for others still there are misunderstandings or incorrect assumptions as to either the status of the *nikah* or the extent to which they believe the law will protect them in the event of a separation (Akhtar, 2015; Vora, 2016b). For some a combination of these factors may be in play, rather than one single determinative

9 See *Akhter v Khan* [2018] EWFC 54; *Attorney General v Akhtar and Khan* [2020] EWCA Civ 122.

reason. With further research we may find other motivations or impediments that deter Muslim couples from entering into legally recognized relationships.

If the framing of this topic is broadened to explore Muslim marriage practices as part of a wider investigation into the multiplicity of ways in which British couples, whether Muslim or not, are forming intimate relationships, and it is investigated as part of the law's response to shifting notions of 'family' then Muslims are not unnecessarily exceptionalized. There are dangers in attempting to find ad hoc solutions to what are perceived to be discrete issues.[10] One can investigate the detailed and varying practices of Muslims in order to fully assess how and why Muslims make choices around the manner in which they enter into intimate relationships, while at the same time paying attention to the wider social and legal developments influencing those practices.

Identifying the state's interest and objectives

In its scoping paper, the Law Commission not only highlighted the 'thriving and largely unregulated market in celebrants conducting non-legally binding marriage ceremonies', but also pointed out that the practice of religious-only marriages has been highlighted within Muslim communities (Law Commission, 2015: 1.34). Further, it advocated for a review of marriage laws, with specific attention to be paid to a number of areas, one of which is the formalities for entry into a state-recognized marriage (1.36).

Before attempting to address how the law should be changed there must be clear key objectives that underpin the rationale for the proposed changes. Probert has noted the cultural, social and linguistic diversity of today's society

10 See https://www.familylaw.co.uk/news_and_comment/criminalising-imams-will-not-solve-the-problem-of-unregistered-marriages (accessed 6 November 2019).

(Probert, 2013). The Law Commission readily accepted that there is a demand for alternative options and a wider range of locations at which marriage ceremonies may be conducted and suggested a thorough review of the law as a whole in order to provide a system that is both coherent and fair to all (1.36). It also set out four key principles by which reform ought to be guided: certainty and simplicity; fairness and equality; protecting the state's interest; respecting individual wishes.

These four guiding principles are important as they indicate what a marriage system should achieve, leaving significant room as to *how* this can be achieved. At the time of writing, the Law Commission has begun its review of the laws around how and where people marry in England and Wales. It has added a fifth guiding principle, that of 'removing of any unnecessary regulation of venues which can hamper choice and increase the cost for couples'.[11] As pointed out by Sandberg, while this review is to be welcomed, the terms of reference appear to indicate limited reform of the law.[12] It would appear that the review will not be carrying out an investigation into the role of marriage as an institution or a wider exploration of adult relationships. In addition, the Law Commission has made it clear it will not make recommendations that might undermine the immigration provisions around 'sham' marriages or the provisions around 'forced' marriages. Nevertheless, there is considerable scope for reform. While the reforms may not challenge why the state chooses to elevate the status of marriage, there is significant scope to improve the current system if we proceed on the assumption that the state ought to

11 Blog post, 'Law Commission begins work on weddings reform', https://www.lawcom.gov.uk/law-commission-begins-work-on-weddings-reform/ (accessed 30 August 2019).

12 Blog post, 'Criminalising imams will not solve the problem of unregistered marriages', https://sandbergrlaw.wordpress.com/2019/07/01/some-initial-thoughts-on-the-law-commissions-project-on-weddings/ (accessed 30 August 2019).

play a role in determining marriage validity. While I concede that there are arguments in favour of severing the state's role completely from determining who is or is not married (Bonthuys, 2016), this chapter is written on the basis that the state will continue to retain an interest in the status of marriage and as such I make proposals for minimal state intervention in relation to the marriage ceremony.

As noted earlier, Muslims marriages can present a challenge for English law, largely due to the ease with which they can be entered into and sometimes the ease with which they are terminated. The interests of the state are not necessarily the same at the point of entry into a relationship as they are at the termination of a relationship (Edge, 2013). At the point of entry I would argue the state's interests lie in establishing the minimum requirements for a valid marriage, ensuring that the state knows who is married and in guarding against marriages of those who are considered incapable whether due to age or other incapacity.[13] Arguably, the state also has an interest in encouraging marriages but none of these interests require the state to dictate the ceremonial aspects of the marriage ceremony (Pywell and Probert, 2018; Probert, 2018c). The state can encourage, recognize and support the institution of marriage without prescribing every aspect of the marriage ceremony.

A proposal for reform: a registered marriage in the true sense

Many times Muslims have been encouraged to 'register' their *nikah* marriages, whether through awareness-raising campaigns, word of mouth, or by mosque or other processes that encourage 'registration' of marriages; it is the language of 'registration' that is often used as part of any awareness-raising campaign (Register Our Marriage campaign; Home Office, 2018). The

---

[13] Law Commission, 2015: 3.7, 3.8; Parveen, 2017.

implication is that 'registration' will allow the parties to convert the *nikah* into a legally recognized relationship. This mistaken notion is referred to by Uddin's participants (Uddin, 2018). In fact, what Muslims are being asked to do is to undertake a separate civil marriage ceremony and comply with all of the necessary legal formalities as though they are not married. There is no method by which Muslims can simply 'register' their *nikahs*. What I am suggesting is the introduction of a registration system that would allow Muslims to register their *nikah* marriages without the necessity for another ceremony. The state provides for the registration of many significant events such as the birth of a child, the death of any human being, the registration of a civil partnership, the establishment of ownership and property rights, and even the registration of rights such as parental responsibility for a child. These rights are created and registered without the state dictating the ceremonial aspects of each. In addition, documentation such as passports and driving licences are all obtained by means of registration systems. Each method of registration has various checks and balances in place to minimize fraud and abuse. Marriage is no more significant as an event and the state should be moving towards a system that allows for the registration of marriages with minimal regulation as to the actual marriage ceremony.

Practicalities

In order to protect against abuse the law can still retain minimum requirements as to who is eligible to marry. In registering the marriage either or both parties may register and they must provide the following:

- full details of the parties together with identification documentation;
- proof of immigration status;
- proof of residency;

- documentary evidence of marriage such as a *nikah* certificate;
- details of the ceremony (date/time/venue) and of the celebrant who conducted the ceremony (if any);
- any change of name documentation if parties' names have been changed;
- name, address and contact details of at least two adult witnesses to the ceremony;
- any other evidence to support the existence of the ceremony such as photographs, videos and so on;
- if either party is divorced or widowed, evidence confirming the same (that is, divorce certificate or death certificate of a former partner);
- (payment of a fee).[14]

The application for registration is to be made online through a centralized system. When the application is received, an officer will carry out the necessary checks to ensure that they are satisfied with the evidence. If the officer has any doubts or concerns they may request further evidence or require the parties or their witnesses to attend a face-to-face interview. Once the officer is satisfied with the evidence, they will post an online notice (and notify the parties) that this marriage will be officially registered after a set period of time. The online notice acts as a public notice and any member of the public may search the online site for these notices. Once the notice period has expired the officer registers the marriage and parties receive an official certificate confirming the same.

If only one party applies for registration then the officer will investigate and allow the other party an opportunity to agree or dispute the registration. A party may only prevent the registration of a marriage if they are arguing that no marriage ceremony took place. If a ceremony has taken place then either party should have the choice to register it. There ought to be

14 I am not advocating a fee, however, it is to be expected that the state will require payment of a fee as it does for registration of any type.

an internal process for dealing with a dispute and if the internal process cannot resolve the dispute then the marriage is not registered and parties may apply to a court to appeal against the decision of the registrar's office. A registered marriage will require a divorce to terminate it.

Notice requirements and the role of an authorized person/ registrar

An online system can still retain the notice periods prior to the registration of marriages albeit *after* the ceremony itself. The online system can in fact provide for a centralized system of notice that is easily accessible by members of the public. More controversial perhaps is the suggestion that a marriage ceremony takes place without an authorized person conducting it or without the presence of a person authorized to register it. It is argued that one of the primary reasons for having an official either conducting or present at marriage ceremonies is that the official can stop a ceremony if they have any concerns as to parties' capacity or concerns around 'sham' or 'forced' marriages. However, one must question whether this is an effective system for the prevention or detection of such marriages. Following a freedom of information request about suspected sham marriages, the Home Office provided the following information:[15] in 2014 it received 3,210 referrals made by Registrars in England and Wales, 2,476 operations were carried out (not all as a result of Registrars' reports), and 1,748 arrests were made. The Home Office was unable to provide any further information so it is not known how many arrests resulted in actual convictions. As a result, there

[15] Freedom of Information Request 34008 response dated 3 February 2015, https://www.whatdotheyknow.com/request/247546/response/613246/attach/3/34008%20Sheppard%20Carradine.pdf?cookie_passthrough=1 (accessed 30 August 2019).

is no real way to ascertain how many actual sham marriages occurred. In the same year there were 247,372 marriages between opposite-sex couples and a further 4,850 marriages between same-sex couples.[16] This means that the reporting of suspected sham marriages by Registrars is, comparatively speaking, only occurring in a very small number of marriage ceremonies. One might query, therefore, whether the use of a registrar or appointed official at every marriage ceremony is the most effective and efficient method for detecting problematic marriages.

Challenges to address

I recognize that a proposal for an online registration system is not without its challenges. In this section I briefly address these.

Unregistered marriages

With the online registration system that I am proposing there are two separate issues to address. First, a marriage may be unregistered due to the registration officer not being satisfied with the evidence that a marriage ceremony has taken place, as a result of which the registration officer refuses to register the marriage. Depending on the reason for refusal it is possible that this decision may be subjected to an appeal before a court. Legislation could set out in clear terms the grounds upon which an appeal may be made, though I recognize that this will need careful framing.

Second, a marriage may be unregistered because parties do not attempt to register it. I do not propose that parties are obligated to register. An unregistered marriage is simply that. It does not attract the legal status of a marriage and nor

16 ONS, 'Marriages in England and Wales: 2014' (ONS, 2017).

does it require a civil divorce to terminate it. It is possible that as part of the provisions of any Cohabitation Bill, parties to an unregistered marriage would automatically qualify for the purposes of the limited financial settlement that may be made available to cohabitees on separation. As mentioned earlier, it is difficult to identify improvements to the legal framework of marriage without placing those improvements within the context of regulating intimate relationships more generally. It is arguable that an unregistered marriage falls somewhere between cohabitation and a legally recognized marriage (Akhtar, 2018a) and therefore may be given the status of a form of cohabitation that is automatically recognized by any forthcoming legislation on cohabitees. Without the introduction of financial protection for cohabitees, parties to an unregistered marriage will either require specific statutory regulation or will find themselves in the same financial legal vacuum currently occupied by cohabitees and parties to a non-qualifying ceremony.

Time period for registration

Another matter to consider is the time period that ought to be available to parties in order to register their marriages. There are obvious advantages to requiring the parties to register within, say, 12 months of the ceremony as it will ensure that evidence is more likely to be available to confirm that a ceremony has taken place. But it is also evident from the case law that often issues around the legal recognition of a marriage do not come to light until the breakdown of the relationship, which may be many years later.[17] In such cases, particularly where hardship may follow, it would be useful if registration were to

[17] Given that there is an absolute bar to commencing divorce proceedings in the first year of a marriage (Matrimonial Causes Act 1973, s 3), it is unlikely that questions as to validity of a marriage will be addressed in the first 12 months.

be permitted outside the set time period. This would need a statutorily regulated discretion.

A religious divorce taking place prior to the registration of a marriage

A final challenge is the impact of any religious or other termination of the marriage prior to registration. This is particularly relevant for Muslim women who may be on the receiving end of unilateral *talaqs* before they have had the opportunity to register their marriages. In effect what is being asked here is whether a religious marriage that has been terminated as far as its religion is concerned can still be legally registered. On the face of it, the answer would appear to be yes. The issues that the law is seeking to promote and protect on marriage recognition are not necessarily the same as those on termination of a relationship. English law can recognize a form of marriage without recognizing particular forms of divorce.[18] The full implications of this would need to be explored in more detail and it is also one of the reasons why limiting the time period within which registration must take place would make sense.

Conclusion

A marriage registration system that makes effective use of technology while minimizing state intervention in the policing of marriage ceremonies will meet the objectives and guiding principles set out by the Law Commission. For Muslims this proposal is based on a notion of partnership

---

18 Indeed, within Islamic scholarship there is far greater disagreement around divorce: the different types, the conditions for each, and the validity and the impact of a specific type of divorce which would justify non-recognition of religious divorces.

between communities and the state. It acknowledges Muslims as 'authors and subjects of more than one legal and cultural system' (Shachar, 2005). Muslims themselves determine how and when they are married and the state gives due recognition to their marriage practices. By removing the state's control over the marriage ceremony the state would give greater freedom to Muslims and non-Muslims alike, allowing them to manage their ceremonies in accordance with their religious or other beliefs. The state would also ensure that the recognition of a marriage is a procedural process rather than state management of a ceremony.

EIGHT

Nikah Ceremonies in the UK: a Tool for Empowerment?

Zainab Naqvi

Introduction

While in recent times, religious-only non-legally recognized Muslim marriages have attracted attention (Law Commission, 2015; Casey 2016; Home Office, 2018), there has been little in-depth engagement with polygynous religious-only marriages. Polygyny is the form of marriage where one man is married to multiple women at the same time (Law Commission, 1971: para 2). It is a recognized form of marriage in many societies worldwide and is considered valid in Islamic law, although some Muslim majority states such as Tunisia have proscribed it. It has been suggested by organizations including the 'Register our Marriage Campaign'[1] that Muslim *nikah* ceremonies should be legally recognized, but this assumes that legal recognition benefits all women equally. In fact, it would limit the autonomy of women who voluntarily opt to live in a religious-only monogamous or polygynous marriage because they see greater benefit in remaining outside of legal recognition. The question arises of how to protect those

[1] See www.registerourmarriage.org (accessed 12 November 2019).

who are vulnerable, while enabling others to enter religious marriages outside of the law.

The solution proposed in this chapter to deal with the varying interests of different women in religious-only marriages is first, that the *nikah* ceremony is legally recognized in principle as a ceremony of marriage. This should be accompanied by the option for both husband and wife to avoid legal recognition through a mutual opt-out process at the point of the religious marriage. Further, if the opt-out is triggered at the time of the ceremony and the religious-only marriage later breaks down, under certain circumstances, it should also be possible to obtain retrospective legal recognition if desired or appropriate in the interests of protecting vulnerable parties.

This proposed legal solution would first create a way for couples to be legally married without needing to undergo another ceremony either before, after, or at the same time as the *nikah* ceremony. It would lead to the *nikah* being a legally recognized form of marriage (although this chapter is not focussed on the form of such recognition). This would tackle the issue of couples' apathy where undergoing an additional legally recognized ceremony at the same or a different time to the religious celebrations, which is seen as burdensome (Akhtar, 2015), and remove any additional costs associated with holding two ceremonies. Further, it would address situations where a promise to complete the legal ceremony is made and then later reneged on by a party.[2]

Polygynous marriages in English law

Currently, under English law it is not permitted to enter a legally recognized polygynous marriage and any such

2 See, for example, *Akhter v Khan* [2018] EWFC 54, *Attorney General v Akhter and Khan* [2020] EWCA Civ 122.

relationship would be void. Furthermore, if you are a citizen or domiciled in the UK and contract a polygynous marriage inside or outside of the UK, such a marriage would also be treated as void.[3]

If an individual is not a UK citizen or domiciled in the UK, it would be possible to contract a polygynous marriage in another state that permits polygyny provided the individual concerned were domiciled there, or in another country that permitted polygamy, at the time. This would be recognized as legally valid in the UK and the English courts would not be prevented from granting matrimonial relief or making a declaration on its validity.[4]

Respecting women's autonomy through mutual registration opt-out

To support women and couples who wish to exercise their autonomy and agency on the question of legal recognition, a mutual opt-out process can be included as a legal requirement to be fulfilled as part of the preliminaries to a religious ceremony. This would require both parties to reach a uniform decision to opt out of legal recognition when signing the *nikah* certificate (or during any other form of religious marriage ceremony). The process of achieving non-legal recognition would thereby become a proactive choice for the parties, overcoming a major issue of inadvertent non-legal recognition. It is worth noting that there are existing ways for couples to protect their financial and other interests if they are not legally married, for example by having a cohabitation agreement in place. Such agreements can be written as formal legal contracts, which would make them binding and enforceable by the

3 Matrimonial Causes Act 1973, s 11(d).

4 Matrimonial Causes Act 1973, s 47(1) as amended by Private International Law (Miscellaneous Provisions) Act 1995, s 5(1).

courts (Probert, 2013: 331). This may not occur frequently in practice but provides another consideration for parties to the *nikah*, and raising awareness of this possibility can only be beneficial for couples.

Of course, there are accounts of men and their families taking advantage of the current religious-only status of the *nikah*, rendering women vulnerable throughout the marriage and its breakdown (Naqvi, 2017b). However, if both parties must opt out of recognition leading up to or during the ceremony, at a rudimentary level this would start a dialogue between the couple and provoke questions for them and their families. A test can be formulated to be applied if a dispute later arises to ensure that consent to not contract a legally recognized marriage was freely given without duress, in accordance with existing English law.[5]

To address the implications of this solution for polygyny, the aim here is to propose a resolution which is conscious of the lack of data around religious-only polygyny's prevalence in the UK as well as what women living in such marriages want and experience (Home Office, 2018: 14–17). It would not be responsible to propose whole-scale legal recognition for the *nikah* without considering the range of relationship types that this could impact upon. The opt-out would have to be triggered in polygynous marriages because there is currently little mainstream appetite for providing any recognition of such marriages. To forcibly create the space for this is inappropriate at this time, not least because it would require reforms of the criminal offence of bigamy, which occurs when an individual has contracted two legally recognized ceremonies.

If such discussions never happen or the power relations between the couple and their families leads to the opt-out being engaged without the full and informed consent of one of the

[5] Matrimonial Causes Act 1973, s 12(1)(c).

parties, an option to seek retrospective legal recognition should be available under very limited circumstances for religious-only monogamous and polygynous marriages. This would require the party seeking recognition to demonstrate that they did not provide full and informed consent; that their religious-only status is being used against them to their detriment; or that they suffered abuse during the marriage, including physical and non-physical forms such as domestic violence and coercive control under section 76 of the Serious Crime Act 2005. This approach would promote a more nuanced, female-centric and responsible way of engaging with religious-only Muslim marriages that respects the autonomy of the women in them. In doing so, the approach would build on recent case law, such as the first instance decision in *Akhter v Khan*, to adopt a more flexible interpretation of the law that accounts for fundamental human rights arguments around the right to marry without interference from the state.[6]

The bigger picture: judicial treatment and non-qualifying ceremony

The statutory approach seems straightforward but does not fully explain what happens in practice. There are instances where a UK-domiciled individual or citizen has celebrated a polygynous marriage overseas and then, for example, the spouse and children from their subsequent marriage have sought entry into the UK.[7] The English courts have acknowledged the existence of the polygynous marriage to prevent the entry of these spouses and children into the country. This has occurred where applicants have sought entry based on their relationship to a British citizen – usually their

---

6 [2018] EWFC 54, [83].

7 See, for example, *R v Immigration Appeal Tribunal ex p Begum (Hasna)* [1995] Imm AR 249; *Azad v Entry Clearance Officer Dhaka* 2000 WL 1918688; *ECO New Delhi v SG* [2012] UKUT 00265 (IAC).

husband or father. Polygyny is used as the basis for denying entry because usually the British citizen has another wife and children already living in the UK. In state welfare cases the courts have also recognized that where a woman or children are from a polygynous household, they cannot access state aid or funds.[8] In such cases, the courts have held, for example, that the wife who is claiming welfare benefits has a husband and therefore someone who should provide for her and their children instead of the state. Such exceptions uphold state interests and are punitive towards polygynous wives.

Additionally, there is another type of polygynous marriage which is often overlooked: non-legally recognized religious-only marriages which are celebrated in the UK (Jaan, 2014; Law Commission, 2015; Casey, 2016; Fairbairn et al, 2017; Home Office, 2018).[9] For a marriage to be legally valid, it must comply with the formalities laid down in the Marriage Act 1949. The Marriage Act 1949 requires that a marriage ceremony be celebrated in a building which is registered for that purpose in the presence of a person authorized to register the marriage (see further Probert, this volume). The Islamic *nikah* is contractual in nature and there is no restriction on location, no need for the contract to be written down and no need for a religious cleric to be present (Akhtar, 2018a: 428).

These differences mean that rather than being void, the *nikah* is a 'non-qualifying ceremony' (Probert, 2013; O'Sullivan and Jackson, 2017; Probert, this volume). Parties to a religious-only Muslim marriage are therefore considered cohabitants or legal strangers (Akhtar, 2018a).

If a Muslim couple want to be legally recognized as married, they can either engage in their legally recognized ceremony at the same time as their *nikah* in the presence of an authorized

---

8 See, for example, *Imam Din v National Assistance Board* [1967] 2 QB 213; *Nabi (Ghulam) v Heaton (Inspector of Taxes)* [1981] 1 WLR 1052; *Bibi v Chief Adjudication Officer* [1998] 1 FLR 375, discussed in Naqvi, 2017a.

9 See also Arbitration and Mediation Services (Equality) Bill [HL] 2016–17.

person in a registered building or have two separate events to solemnize the *nikah* and the legal marriage (Probert and Saleem, 2018). This separation between religious and legal recognition means couples can undergo the *nikah* ceremony while remaining legal strangers or cohabitants in English law if they so choose.

Women engaging in religious-only marriages: research findings

There is little research focussed primarily on Muslim religious-only marriages and polygyny specifically, and in the UK most of the existing research findings are periphery issues in projects focussed on Muslim divorce, Sharia Councils and community integration (Law Commission, 2015; Casey, 2016; Home Office, 2018). However, any solution to the 'problem' with religious-only Muslim marriage must account for this relationship type.

Unsurprisingly, religious-only marriages are highlighted in Sharia Council research because the main role of these Councils is to provide women with a route to seeking the dissolution of their *nikah* when their husband is uncooperative (Parveen, 2017). For women who have no access to formal legal remedies, there may be no other option but to apply to a Sharia Council for a solution.

In one of the earlier studies of Sharia Councils in the UK, Shah-Kazemi (2001) studied hundreds of Council case files to find that approximately 27 per cent of users did not appear to have legally recognized marriages. Further, five of the 21 women she interviewed for her report were also not in valid English marriages (Shah-Kazemi, 2001: 31). The prevalence of polygynous marriage in the data was extremely low, with an estimated 1.2 per cent of the case files concerning this (Shah-Kazemi, 2001: 31).

A few years later, Douglas et al reported that 14 of 27 Birmingham Central Mosque Sharia Council hearings observed by the researchers had pertained to *nikah*-only marriages (Douglas et al, 2012), while Bano found that only nine of the 25 women she had interviewed regarding their experiences of using Sharia Councils had been in legally recognized marriages (Bano, 2004: 221). Of the remaining 16 participants who were not married in English law, 12 were intentionally misled to believe that they would have a legal ceremony at a later date; two incorrectly believed that they had legal recognition and two intentionally remained religious-only (Bano, 2004: 221). Vora's small-scale qualitative study of religious-only wives had similar findings, with two of the ten religious-only wives he interviewed consciously avoiding legal recognition of their relationship (Vora, 2016b). In the same vein, Parveen and Uddin have respectively conducted studies on Sharia Councils and Muslim women's experiences of divorce, finding that there is a noticeable number of Muslim couples contracting religious-only marriages. Parveen examined 100 case files from a Sharia Council in London and 29 were religious-only. Again, there were a small number of polygynous marriage cases evidencing a need to engage with this minority form of religious-only marriage (Parveen, 2018a). Through his qualitative interviews with women, Uddin also noted the diverse range of perspectives and experiences on religious-only marriages which include polygyny (Uddin, 2018).

As well as academic interest, Sharia Councils have attracted significant media and political attention. From Baroness Cox's Arbitration and Mediation Services (Equality) Bill [HL] 2016–17 seeking to regularize and limit the role and power of Sharia Councils, to the recent *Independent review into the application of sharia law in England and Wales* (Home Office, 2018) that examined the Councils as part of the government's counter-terrorism strategy, the 'problem' of religious-only marriages has been raised – feeding into a larger debate on the compatibility of Islam and its values with English law and society (Casey, 2016; Hanna and Lowes, 2018: 133). It is important to ensure that any critical examination of religious-only marriage and polygyny does not perpetuate sensationalized and essentialized views of Muslim communities and their practices. The dangers of this are represented in the Casey Review on Integration and Equality of Opportunity (2016). The Review argues that the prevalence of religious-only marriage in any group is an alarming indication that people are not accessing their rights. Interestingly, this is argued without reference to the fact that cohabitation is the fastest-growing form of relationship in the UK (ONS, 2019). Religious-only wives are in the same legal position as cohabitants, which means that portraying religious-only Muslim wives as especially vulnerable without reflecting the same level of concern for cohabitants is unbalanced (see Akhtar, this volume).

The Casey Review further asserts that the practice of religious-only polygyny is more commonplace than one might think though this statement is based on 'accusations, anecdotes and assertions encountered throughout our engagement' (Casey, 2016: para 8.45), which is vague. The meaning of 'more commonplace than one might think' (Casey, 2016: para 8.45) is not clarified and appears to be alarmist and based on limited unscientific evidence.

Adopting a more measured approach, in 2015 the Law Commission underlined the need for further exploration of Muslim religious-only marriages, which includes thinking through the implications of legal responses for women in Muslim polygynous marriages. Inspired by this burgeoning attention, a documentary was produced for Channel 4 television entitled *The Truth About Muslim Marriage*. The programme shared the results of the largest survey on Muslim marriage in the UK so far with 903 respondents. It was discovered that 60 per cent of the women surveyed were in a religious-only marriage, with approximately 11 per cent of them being polygynous (True Vision, 2017). During the programme, one of the researchers raised the question of polygyny, alluding to the idea that religious-only polygynous wives with whom she had spoken were not happy with legal recognition because it may prevent their practice of polygyny (True Vision, 2017).

This figure of just over 10 per cent of the 903 women surveyed living as polygynous wives indicates that more exploration and research are needed into the prevalence of polygyny as well as a legal approach which is responsive to these women's right to autonomy over their lifestyle choices and relationships.

What are the benefits of being legally married?

Women in religious-only marriages are vulnerable when the relationship breaks down, either through death or divorce. The vulnerability is acute where they are economically reliant on the spouse (O'Sullivan and Jackson, 2017: 25) because they are treated as cohabitants, which has several consequences.

First, unlike the wife in a valid or void marriage, they cannot have access to the family courts to seek a divorce or financial remedies.[10] In *The Truth About Muslim Marriage*, contesting or proving property ownership was highlighted as one of the main difficulties that women face on relationship breakdown (True Vision, 2017). While it may be possible to claim ownership rights under the principle of proprietary estoppel or a common intention constructive trust (O'Sullivan and Jackson, 2017: 26), it is extremely hard to satisfy the requirements for these (see Miles, this volume).

Second, there is no automatic recognition for the purposes of inheritance. For example, in *Ghandi v Patel*,[11] a widow who had married her husband as a second wife in a Hindu ceremony conducted by a Brahmin priest in an Indian restaurant was not able to inherit from her husband's estate. The consequences would have been the same if the marriage had been monogamous.

10 Matrimonial Causes Act 1973, ss 23 and 24.

11 [2001] EWHC Ch 473.

Similarly, there is generally no guaranteed access for a religious-only wife to her deceased husband's pension and state welfare aid.[12] In the case of polygynous marriages, if one wife is legally recognized and subsequent wives are religious-only, this will lead to one wife being eligible to receive the pension over the others. There have been cases in which cohabitants were considered entitled to benefits such as their deceased spouse's pension.[13] This shift is quite recent and as decisions are made on a case-by-case basis, there is no guarantee that this entitlement would be upheld in every instance.

With regard to immigration, the protection of public interests is still prioritized. Without registration, one may enter the UK on a fiancé(e) visa, but a legally recognized marriage is required for leave to remain. For women in polygynous marriages, even with a legally recognized marriage that was celebrated in a polygyny-permitting jurisdiction, entry would be denied if there were another wife already resident in the UK.[14] Moreover, children of polygynous marriages contracted abroad are not permitted entry into the UK because it is considered better for the child to remain overseas.[15]

There are also implications for parental responsibility. When parents are in a legally recognized marriage, the mother's husband is assumed to be a parent under section 2(1) of the Children Act 1989. If the marriage is not legally recognized, this is not the case and because religious-only marriages are non-qualifying ceremonies section 1(1) of the Legitimacy Act

---

12 *Chief Adjudication Officer v Bath* [2000] 1 FLR 8; *Bibi v Chief Adjudication Officer* [1998] 1 FLR 375.

13 See, for example, *R (Elmes) v Essex CC* [2019] 1 WLR 1686.

14 *R v Immigration Appeal Tribunal ex p Begum (Hasna)* [1995] Imm AR 249; *RB v UK (Bibi v UK)* App No 19628/92, ECmHR decision of 29 June 1992; *MS (Somalia) v Secretary of State for the Home Department* [2010] Imm AR 242.

15 *Azad v Entry Clearance Officer Dhaka* [2001] INLR 109; *ECO New Delhi v SG* [2012] UKUT 00265 (IAC).

1976 does not apply either.[16] This means that in order to be registered as the father of a child, both parents have to sign the birth register together; one parent must complete a statutory declaration of parentage form, which is presented at the time of birth registration, or the birth is registered with a document from the court which gives the father parental responsibility.[17] This makes the process significantly more onerous.

Being disruptive: the religious-only *nikah* as a tool for empowerment?

Based on the previous discussion, a legally recognized ceremony of marriage seems to be the ideal way to protect individual rights. However, there are some benefits to avoiding legal recognition.

First, there is evidence to suggest that religious-only Muslim marriages are not always the product of bad intentions. Akhtar's research has uncovered some interesting trends. Cohabitation outside marriage is not accepted in Islam and so Muslim couples live together only after marriage. However, it is important to consider what we mean by being married here. Is legal recognition the only way to validate your marital status? Akhtar's survey of Muslim couples living in religious-only *nikah* marriages shows that reasons for not seeking legal recognition can vary, from viewing the legal ceremony as low priority, to wanting to experiment with a live-in relationship while adhering to religious norms (Akhtar, 2018a: 447). In this way, a religious-only marriage provides the space for women to experience cohabitation and conduct their relationship outside of state-determined boundaries.

Women can also use the religious-only *nikah* to disrupt stigmas around cohabitation, divorce and polygyny to empower

16 *AAA v ASH* [2009] EWHC 636 (Fam).

17 Children Act 1989, s 4.

themselves and live in a relationship arrangement which suits them. In previous research, these themes have emerged with regard to the *nikah* and polygyny (Naqvi, 2017b). For example, in one woman's case, she fell in love with someone who was already married and chose to live in a religious-only polygynous marriage with the expectation that her rights as a wife would be fulfilled regardless of her legal status. This arrangement permitted her to challenge the stigma around her divorces and those who reinforce them by demonstrating that the perceived barriers to marriage for divorced women in her community did not prevent her from marrying the man she loves (Naqvi, 2017b).

In another case, the woman did not undergo the legally recognized ceremony because her husband was 'anti-secular' and considered the religious ceremony legally binding. It was possible that they would later undergo their legally recognized marriage. Her experiences raised another interesting possibility for the use of the *nikah*. The *nikah* is contractual in nature, meaning its terms and contents are open to negotiation between the couple. This woman had taken advantage of this and had negotiated the insertion of clauses pertaining to her husband supporting her ambition to become a doctor and preventing him from practising polygyny while married to her (Read, 2012: 453–4; Naqvi, 2017b). This level of autonomous negotiation of marriage terms is not available as part of the formal, official process of getting married in English law at present because it is assumed that it already exists. Providing the opportunity for such open discussion between the two parties is helpful if they wish to take advantage of it. In existing law, pre-nuptial and *mahr* agreements are examples of contracts that have been entertained in the English courts and therefore give couples the opportunity to record discussions around the rights and consequences of being in the marriage. This shows that the courts have the capacity to deal with contracts around marriage, demonstrating the potential to see marriage as a contract itself.

Finally, in terms of more practical benefits, existing research has found examples of some women deliberately avoiding legal recognition to protect their assets (Bano, 2004; Akhtar, 2015; Vora, 2016b). Here, instead of wives being denied ownership of the marital home and other financial remedies, they are actively protecting their own property by refusing to legally marry. While it is recognized that this is in the minority of cases, blanket registration would take away that choice for women and their ability to disrupt the stereotype of their always being the weaker party. Religious-only marriages can provide women with a way of upholding their beliefs while empowering them to protect their assets.

Conclusion

In this chapter it has been demonstrated through using the case study of polygynous Muslim marriages that there are benefits and disadvantages to being in both legally recognized and religious-only marriages. The autonomy of religious-only and legally recognized wives can both be upheld and interfered with through the relationship and its breakdown and so blanket legal recognition for Muslim *nikah* ceremonies is not desirable, not least because of the confusion and complexities it would cause for women who choose to be in a polygynous marriage. A responsible and realistic approach which accounts for the lack of research on polygyny would be to legally recognize Muslim monogamous marriages unless both parties opt out of this. It is intended that this solution would instigate the necessary conversations as to what marriage is in English law and how its breakdown should be regulated in a way which supports and advances the autonomy of Muslim women and their relationship choices.

NINE

In Pursuit of an Islamic Divorce: a Socio-Legal Examination of Practices Among British Muslims

Islam Uddin

Introduction

Existing studies demonstrate how some British Muslims follow customary/normative laws from their cultures of origin, resulting in marriage performed according to religious rites only. Where this is not coupled with a civil ceremony of marriage, these couples are treated as cohabitants by the law, and their *nikah* is seen as a 'non-qualifying ceremony' or 'non-existent marriage', limiting their access to state dispute resolution mechanisms. This paves the way for religious dispute resolution forums such as Sharia Councils. Recent debates have focused on the use of Sharia Councils as quasi-legal, unofficial bodies that function to mediate, arbitrate and issue Islamic divorce certificates. Critics argue that Sharia Councils follow Islamic norms, discriminate against Muslim women, operate as a parallel legal system and contradict human rights law and therefore should be banned. Others view Sharia Councils as flexible and providing a solution to the needs of users, mainly

Muslim women, while operating within the law. The 2018 *Independent review into the application of sharia law in England and Wales* recommended regulation of Sharia Councils (Home Office, 2018).

This chapter explores the practices of Islamic marriages and divorce among British Muslims, providing a valuable insight into the intricacy of such practices. It also examines formal and informal dispute resolution mechanisms; dimensions of inequality, discrimination, agency, and access to justice in the use of Sharia Councils and other dispute resolution forums; and the plurality of solutions formulated within Muslim communities. This chapter suggests the need to establish a 'standard of practice' among those forums that provide services to Muslim women seeking Islamic divorce in order to safeguard and empower women and address any imbalances arising from norms that disadvantage Muslim women.

Muslim family law: background

Muslim family law has multiple forms. One interpretation is that it represents those aspects of Sharia law (that is, Islamic law) that govern marriage, divorce, maintenance, child custody, and inheritance (An-Naim, 2002: xi). Some argue that in the minds of many British Muslims, being faithful to their religion means following what was customary in their country of origin (Ramadan, 2004), including marriage and divorce, and thus apply Sharia law in a personal capacity (An-Naim, 2010). Others argue that there should be one law applicable to all citizens and that there is no place for Sharia law in Britain (MacEoin, 2009). One argument against its use is the claim that Muslim women are coerced into using Sharia Councils (Namazie et al, 2010).

In light of such opposing discourses, this chapter presents some findings of research examining the practices of Islamic marriages and divorce among British Muslims. Beginning with a brief background to the study and the reason for the research, it then discusses the lived experience of divorce among the participants and highlights the significance of obtaining Islamic divorces. The next section discusses the role of Sharia Councils in facilitating Islamic divorce and suggests practical solutions to improve the service provision. It concludes with a discussion on the importance of Islamic divorce.

In the UK, Sharia Councils as dispute resolution forums face criticism on numerous grounds. Primarily, the way in which Islamic laws are interpreted and applied, resulting in the marginalization of women and favourable terms for men, is a key issue (Bano, 2007; Ahmed and Norton, 2012). In 2016 the Casey Review claimed there was evidence of discriminatory practices among Sharia Councils that disadvantaged Muslim women (Casey, 2016). Similarly, in May 2016, Baroness Cox introduced a Private Members' Bill on the application of equality legislation to arbitration and mediation services. This was seen as attempting to address the problems of inequality within Sharia Councils; however, the bill did not progress past its second hearing in the House of Lords in January 2017 (Arbitration and Mediation Services (Equality) Bill [HL] 2016–17). Opposing such criticisms, others have found that Sharia Councils have a flexible approach, encourage couples to enter legally binding marriage and divorce (Bowen, 2016: 212) and do not seek state recognition, while also confirming religious divorces, which are spiritually meaningful to female users and not accessible from the state (Douglas et al, 2011). *The independent review into the application of sharia law in England and Wales*, while critical, nonetheless recognized that these bodies are performing an essential role and recommended that Sharia Councils be regulated to help overcome the mounting criticisms (Home Office, 2018).

The research referenced in this chapter involved interviewing British Muslim women and experts or professionals such as imams, Sharia Council judges, solicitors and counsellors, who had been identified as providing services to Muslim women during their marriages, marital disputes and divorce. Sharia

Council hearings were also observed and their procedural documents analysed. The findings provide a valuable insight into marriage and divorce among British Muslims. The remainder of this chapter discusses the lived experience of religious divorce among British Muslims and then examines Sharia Councils and advocates for a 'standard of practice' to safeguard women who use their services.

Religious divorce among British Muslims

Under Muslim family law, Islamic divorce can take many forms, these being *talaq*, *tafwid*, *khula*, *mubarah* and *faskh*.[1] *Talaq* refers to the husband's unilateral divorce, whereas *tafwid*, *khula* and *mubarah* are means for the wife to be released from the marriage, and *faskh* is the dissolution of the marriage by a Sharia authority (Esposito and DeLong-Bas, 2001; Arshad, 2010). The two most common forms of divorce are *talaq* and *khula*. A key difference between the two is that, in the case of *talaq*, the husband must ensure full payment of the *mahr*[2] to the wife, whereas with *khula*, the wife requests a divorce and in turn may have to return the *mahr* to the husband. *Talaq* is thus financially more advantageous for women. Both of these procedures can be extrajudicial, meaning the husband and wife can respectively pronounce *talaq* or *khula* and complete their religious divorce without the intervention of a Sharia authority. However, this study found that some participants still referred *talaq* and *khula* to a Sharia Council for authoratative confirmation. Two of the participants explained the circumstances that led to their Islamic divorce being referred to a Sharia Council.

1 *Talaq* (husband's unilateral divorce), *tafwid* (delegated power of divorce from the husband to the wife), *khula* (wife initiated divorce), *mubarah* (mutual agreement to divorce), and *faskh* (dissolution by a Sharia authority).

2 *Mahr* (dower – a gift or provision from the husband to the wife).

> 'He [the husband] approached the Shariah Council, not me. He wanted a certificate, as he intended to go abroad and remarry. When the Shariah Council called me to say my husband had applied for *talaq*. I told them, he has already divorced me.' (Rupa)

> 'I asked him [the husband] for the divorce certificate [that is, *khula*] from the Shariah Council. He wasn't bothered, but he gave it a year later. I needed it to move on. I needed it as proof my first marriage ended for any potential groom.' (Kulsuma)

Participants with legally binding marriages invariably applied for civil divorce. In some instances these women tried to pursue an Islamic divorce first; however, faced with resistance from their husbands, the women decided to petition for a civil divorce, as one participant explained: "I wanted the courts to deal with him. He was violent and harassing me [after separation], stalking me at work. My family was stalling the civil divorce process as they wanted the Islamic divorce first, but he was not agreeing, so I chose the civil [divorce] path" (Inaya).

However, civil law falls short of resolving religious divorce. The civil proceedings may not dissolve the religious part of the marriage, and this, in turn, creates a problem for Muslim women who are now faced with the prospect of pursuing an Islamic divorce outside the state legal system. There are several reasons why Muslims will seek an Islamic divorce in spite of having a civil divorce certificate. The participants in this study expressed the view that religious divorce was important to them as it severed the religiously recognized marital relationship and contact with the husband and his family, removed any doubts as to whether the women were still married, and allowed women the freedom to move on, and remarry if they wished. As the civil divorce proceeding does not resolve the religious marriage, women who are unable to attain an Islamic divorce can find themselves in a limping marriage, whereby legally they are divorced but are still seen as married by some members of the Muslim community until they achieve an Islamic divorce (Pearl and Menski, 1998).

Participants mentioned that the plurality of views among the different religious 'Schools of Thought'[3] as to how to enact *talaq*, *khula* and *faskh* created much confusion. For example, did a civil divorce also count as a religious divorce or not? Some Sharia Councils accepted a civil divorce as sufficient evidence to grant a religious divorce without further investigation, while others required applicants to file for an Islamic divorce. The majority of participants who had gained a civil divorce found their husbands withheld the religious divorce. In trying to resolve the issue of Islamic divorce, Sharia Councils were not the obvious first choice as a point of reference. Rather, in practice, Muslim women only turned to imams, the mosque or Sharia Councils after other means to resolve the issue of Islamic divorce had failed, as one imam explained: "People come to the imam or the mosque after they have tried on their own to rectify the situation. They would incorporate their family and trusted friends. The last resort would be the imam" (Imam #1). In fact, the majority of women in this study who had obtained a civil divorce achieved an Islamic divorce without the need to turn to a Sharia Council. This was mainly due to two reasons. Some participants, after enquiry, accepted that their civil divorce was sufficient, while others believed a long separation in addition to a civil divorce certificate was sufficient. However, despite reaching such conclusions, participants mentioned the difficulty in verifying their Islamic divorce. One participant explained how she disregarded her local mosque and opted to accept an informal process of verification.

[3] Schools of Thoughts, that is, *madhhabs*, are schools of Islamic jurisprudence, named after their founding scholars, for example, Hanafi, Maliki, Shafi'i and Hanbali.

> 'I went to the mosque and asked for an Islamic divorce. The imam tried to patch things up, I said, "Even after I've been through DV?" He said, "DV is not a good enough reason". My brother said, "Come on, let's go, you've got a civil divorce and that's enough". I asked my neighbour's sister who is a Quran *hafiz*.[4] She asked someone, who said three months *iddah*[5] period is enough.' (Salma)

For Salma, verification that the conditions of an Islamic divorce had been met, rather than following a due process with a Sharia Council, was sufficient in the light of also having a civil divorce. However, for women in religious *nikah*-only marriages, Sharia Councils may be the only option in gaining an Islamic divorce.

The role of Sharia Councils

Sharia Councils are quasi-legal, unofficial bodies that function to mediate, arbitrate and issue Islamic divorce certificates (Bano, 2012). There are many factors that contribute to the existence of Sharia Councils in Britain, such as the Muslim community upholding and applying family laws from their countries of origin, or the need for Sharia law from a Muslim community public interest (*maslahah*) perspective. Perhaps the most important factor is simply that Muslim women turn to Sharia Councils for their services, as one professional explained:

> 'Ninety per cent of our cases are women initiated divorce. Women come to us because they want verification that they are divorced because their husband pronounced divorce, or they started the civil

4 The *hafiz* is a person who has memorized the Quran.

5 The *iddah* is a nominated period of time which a woman must wait before she can be pronounced divorced or widowed or can remarry.

> proceedings and want the Islamic divorce. In other cases, women have no civil marriage and come to us [Shariah Council] as they have nowhere else to go to get a divorce.' (SC Judge #1)

Sharia Councils face criticism that women who use their services are discriminated against, having to pay higher fees than men, wait for a lengthier divorce process, and being pressured to reconcile with violent husbands (Casey, 2016). Furthermore, there are no independent mechanisms to monitor Sharia Councils, clients do not have access to legal advice or representation, proceedings are not recorded, nor are there any recorded judgments or any rights to appeal decisions (Namazie et al, 2010). Concerns are expressed that Muslim women concede their civil rights and agree to a weaker bargaining position using Sharia law (Manea, 2016; Walker, 2016). Others contend that Muslim women are aware of the contested rulings of religious scholars, and of their rights under civil law, and that they are able to challenge their weak bargaining position in the marriage during negotiations at the Sharia Councils (Bano, 2013).

The independent review into the application of sharia law in England and Wales found evidence of good and bad practices among Sharia Councils, however the variance in the practices and standards led to the report recommending that the state intervene to create a body to design a system of self-regulation of Sharia Councils, and to ensure the effective monitoring of compliance (Home Office, 2018). The government rejected this proposal and did not consider there to be a role for the state to act in this way as it could add legitimacy to the perceived existence of a parallel legal system.[6]

Previous studies of marital breakdown among British Muslims found that the bulk of the cases dealt with by Sharia

6 Amber Rudd, Written Statement, HCSW442, 1 February 2018.

Councils were *faskhs*[7] (Qureshi, 2016). The findings from this study indicate that Sharia Councils have to resort to declaring *faskh* due to the unwillingness of men to release women from marriage, as explained by one of the Sharia Council judges:

> 'It is an affront to men if a woman remarries; it is like how dare she move on. Men are withholding *talaq* or refusing to grant *khula* even though the wife has every right to it. In one case, the man had separated from his wife two years ago. So why does he not give her *talaq*? He withholds the *talaq* out of spite. The man gets annoyed if someone else can issue a divorce certificate, as it means he cannot be spiteful to her anymore.' (SC Judge #1)

In this function alone, Sharia Councils fulfil an important role in freeing Muslim women from limping marriages, something civil authorities are unable to provide. One participant who had a *nikah*-only marriage explained her situation:

> 'My husband said he was never going to give me an Islamic divorce. So I asked my cousin what to do. He is a *hafiz* [memorized Quran], he said, "apply to the Shariah Council they will help you." So, I applied to the Shariah Council. I thought the fee was too much, and they said that the process could take up to 6–9 months. My application took longer than this to process and the certificate was delayed. But in the end, they understood me and agreed to dissolve the marriage, which they did.' (Jahanara)

Despite finding the application process cumbersome, this participant accepted that ultimately the Sharia Council was able

7 *Faskh* (dissolution by a Sharia authority).

to resolve her Islamic divorce. However, another participant mentioned how she stopped her application with the Sharia Council upon receiving her civil divorce. Thus, the need for verification of Islamic divorce from a Sharia Council is based upon personal conviction as well as religious requirements.

In general, the professionals interviewed felt that Sharia Councils contributed in a positive way by securing Islamic divorce for Muslim women, though they accepted not all Sharia Councils processed divorce efficiently and there was scope to improve their procedures and infrastructure. In particular, they felt the time to process *khula* cases should be reduced, especially where the husband delays proceedings without reason. Moreover, the professionals agreed there was a need for greater female representation at Sharia Councils, ranging from caseworkers to board members.

While Sharia Councils are imperfect in their current form, with great room for improvement, they currently fill a void in civil law provision by settling religious divorce and therefore fulfil a need in the Muslim community. Thus, the findings of this study suggest the need to establish a 'standard of practice' to ensure equality and justice among forums that provide services to Muslim women seeking Islamic divorce. In the first instance, forums that recognize a civil divorce as sufficient and issue an Islamic divorce certificate accordingly would seem to represent the best option for Muslim women seeking religious divorce. Secondly, there needs to be equality in the divorce application process, whereby the fees charged for men and women are the same, and the length of time to process applications is consistent, clear and transparent. Thirdly, these forums need to incorporate a complaints procedure and appeals system in respect of the decisions given, in order to ensure justice and transparency. Fourthly, female representation is required at different levels of the application process, from female caseworkers to female members on the Sharia board or decision-making panel. Adopting these recommendations would ensure Sharia Councils and other similar forums safeguard and empower women and address any imbalances arising from norms that disadvantage Muslim women.

Conclusion

This chapter examined the lived realities of marriage and divorce experiences of British Muslims and highlighted the importance of Islamic religious divorce to end a marriage. The process of civil divorce has some relevance to the religious divorce process, becoming significant for those Muslim women and Sharia Councils who accept it as evidencing religious divorce. However, for many women and some Sharia Councils, the religious processes supersede any civil process, and therefore the solutions proposed in this chapters seek to improve standards among forums that provide services to Muslim women seeking Islamic divorce.

TEN

Arbitration as a Legal Solution for Relationship Breakdown in the Muslim Community: the Case of the Muslim Arbitration Tribunal

Amin Al-Astewani

Introduction

This chapter argues that family arbitration represents a promising legal solution for relationship breakdown in religious communities such as the Muslim community. This is particularly so in light of two recent developments which have opened up new avenues in the field of family arbitration, namely the official introduction of a Family Arbitration Scheme in England and Wales, and the novel precedent established in the 2013 case of *AI v MT*.[1] Following an analysis of these two developments, this chapter highlights the case of the Muslim Arbitration Tribunal as an arguably successful model which indicates the feasibility and potential of family arbitration in disputes involving religious marriages.

Religious marriages may or may not be legally recognized, depending on the extent to which they have also engaged with the requirements of the civil law (see Probert, Vora,

1 *AI v MT* [2013] EWHC 100.

Parveen, this volume). If they are not recognized, alternative methods of dispute resolution, such as family arbitration, become particularly pertinent in regulating relationship breakdown because they may represent the only legal avenue for dispute resolution in such cases. On the other hand, even if religious marriages are legally recognized, a civil court is unable to engage with the religious sensitivities involved on the breakdown of such marriages in the same way that an alternative dispute resolution mechanism, such as family arbitration, has the capacity to do, as this chapter will attempt to illustrate.

The Arbitration Act 1996

The Arbitration Act 1996 is the main piece of legislation regulating arbitration in England and Wales. It was principally created in order to provide the commercial community with an adequate means of privately resolving their disputes (Hunter, 1987: 195). In this regard the Act sought to reconcile two conflicting interests in arbitration as an alternative method of dispute resolution (Redfern, 1986; Chukwumerije, 1999). The first was the interest of private parties in a swift, inexpensive and decisive resolution to their disputes outside of court. The second was the interest of the legal system in ensuring that the fairness, impartiality and integrity of the process were fully secured.

Section 1 of the Act explicitly expresses the legislation's intent to reconcile such interests. It stipulates that the object of arbitration is 'to obtain the fair resolution of disputes by an impartial tribunal without unnecessary delay or expense' and that parties are 'free to agree how their disputes are resolved, subject only to such safeguards as are necessary in the public interest'.[2] The Act allows parties to select the arbitrator who

[2] Arbitration Act 1996, s 1.

will decide the dispute and the arbitral procedure.[3] More pertinently, it allows the parties to select the law to be applied by the arbitrator in reaching their decision.[4] This, as recent case law has affirmed,[5] extends to religious law such as Jewish and Islamic law. The Act also conferred legal status on the decisions of arbitrators by making their decisions binding on the parties, and severely limited the ability of the parties to appeal such decisions.[6]

The Act did not overlook the interest of the state in overseeing the process and ensuring that it was conducted as fairly and judiciously as possible. Section 33 imposes a duty on arbitrators 'to act fairly and impartially as between the parties'.[7] Sections 67 and 68 also provide that arbitration decisions which do not comply with minimal standards of fairness and due process or which fall foul of public policy can be quashed by the courts upon a challenge made by one of the parties.[8] Arbitrators were also limited to deciding civil disputes, with criminal and divorce proceedings remaining beyond their jurisdiction.[9] A criminal dispute in English law is between the defendant and the Crown, and not between civil parties. It is therefore not possible for civil parties to agree to arbitration in the case of a breach of the criminal law (Blacklett, 2009: 13). A religious arbitration tribunal which attempted to enforce a physical criminal sanction would itself be liable for breaching state law (Blacklett, 2009: 14).

3 Arbitration Act 1996, ss 3, 16, 34.

4 Arbitration Act 1996, s 46.

5 See, for example, *Kohn v Wagschal & Ors* [2007] EWCA Civ 1022.

6 Arbitration Act 1996, s 58(1).

7 Arbitration Act 1996, s 33.

8 Arbitration Act 1996, ss 67, 68.

9 As Knights notes, '[a]s regards other areas of law, the English courts are not bound to enforce any order made by a religious court within the United Kingdom other than orders made by the courts of the Church of England' (Knights, 2007: 76).

The role of arbitration is also limited under family law (Centre for Social Cohesion, 2009: 17). Since the establishment of judicial divorce in the 19th century, English law has asserted an exclusive legal jurisdiction in the welfare of the child whose parents become divorced, as well as the financial consequences of the divorce (Douglas, 2015: 57). This does not preclude private arbitration tribunals such as religious tribunals judging on matters relating to divorce, for example financial settlement and the welfare of the children involved. It simply means such judgments will have no legal effect unless they are approved by the courts via an order known as a consent order. Within the context of a family law case involving the potential for religious arbitration, Baker J has stated:

> In considering the parties' proposals to refer the dispute to arbitration, the following legal principles were of particular relevance. First, insofar as the court has jurisdiction to determine issues arising out of the marriage, or concerning the welfare and upbringing of the children, that jurisdiction cannot be ousted by agreement. The parties cannot lawfully make an agreement either not to invoke the jurisdiction or to control the powers of the court where jurisdiction in invoked: see Lord Hailsham in *Hyman v Hyman* [1929] AC 601.[10]

The Family Arbitration Scheme

Although the Arbitration Act did not explicitly exclude family disputes from arbitration, this was not formally considered by family judges and lawyers for over a decade, largely due to the historical monopolization of marital disputes by the

---

[10] *AI v MT* [2013] EWHC at [26]–[27]. See also Hansard [HL] Nov 2008 WA81.

English courts, as mentioned earlier. A number of subsequent developments, however, led to a gradual shift in attitudes, culminating in the eventual embrace of family arbitration. The first was a growing respect accorded by English judges to the personal autonomy of parties involved in marital disputes. This was manifested in the landmark case of *Radmacher v Granatino*,[11] which established that agreements which parties have come to themselves for the determination of their financial affairs following divorce would be given effect in the absence of overriding public policy concerns. As Lord Philips stated:

> The reason why the court should give weight to a nuptial agreement is that there should be respect for individual autonomy. The court should accord respect to the decision of a married couple as to the manner in which their financial affairs should be regulated. It would be paternalistic and patronising to override their agreement simply on the basis that the court knows best. This is particularly true where the parties' agreement addresses existing circumstances and not merely the contingencies of an uncertain future.[12]

The significance of *Granatino* was succinctly captured by Charles J in the 2012 case of *V v V*:

> [*Granatino's* case] necessitates a significant change to the approach to be adopted, on a proper application of the discretion conferred by the [Matrimonial Causes Act 1973], to the impact of agreements between the parties in respect of their finances. At the heart of that

11 [2010] UKSC 42, at [78].

12 [2010] UKSC 42, at [78]. It should be noted that the courts will give greater weight to an agreement entered into after separation than to a pre-nuptial agreement, as the last sentence of Lord Philips' statement indicates.

> significant change, is the need to recognise the weight that should now be given to autonomy, and thus to the choices made by the parties to a marriage … The new respect to be given to individual autonomy means that the fact of an agreement can alter what is a fair result and so found a different award to the one that would otherwise have been made.[13]

The second development was a more concerted effort by the family courts to encourage parties to settle their matrimonial disputes privately rather than become entangled in adversarial litigation (Douglas, 2015: 61).[14] This principle became firmly enshrined in English law in 2010, with the Family Procedure Rules obliging courts to encourage parties to use an alternative dispute resolution procedure if the court considers this appropriate.[15] Inextricably linked to this development and without doubt one of its key catalysts was the fact that the family court system has become so overburdened it has almost reached breaking point (Kennett, 2016: 4–5). The third relevant development was the successful introduction of family arbitration in other prominent common law jurisdictions including the US, Canada and Australia (Kennett, 2016: 1–2).

These developments coalesced in 2012 with the official launch in England and Wales of a Family Arbitration Scheme by the newly formed Institute of Family Law Arbitrators (IFLA) (Ferguson, 2013: 116). This scheme was formally endorsed in 2014 by the President of the Family Division, Sir James Munby,[16] who subsequently issued official practice

13 *V v V (Prenuptial Agreement)* [2012] 1 FLR 1315, at [36].

14 It should be noted that these efforts had been ongoing for some time, with the Family Law Act 1996 requiring spouses seeking divorce to attend a preliminary Information Session and to seek mediation as a first step, see Family Law Act 1996, Part II.

15 The Family Procedure Rules 2010, r 3(2).

16 In *S v S* [2014] EWHC 7 (Fam).

guidance concerning arbitration in the family courts.[17] The scheme took into consideration the special nature of marital disputes and tailored the arbitration process to distinguish it from the standard form of arbitration under the 1996 Act in two important ways.

The first was that family arbitration would not be legally binding, but rather would require a consent order from the family court in order to be judicially approved and enforceable, although the President of the Family Division stated that consent orders will only be refused in the very rarest of cases.[18] This is in keeping with the traditional position of the courts on the private resolution of marital disputes and ensures judicial oversight of the process. The second is that only English law may be applied in such arbitration, excluding the possibility of foreign laws, including religious law, being applied.[19] The scheme had initially also limited the scope of family arbitration to financial and property disputes, excluding disputes related to the care and parenting of children. This changed in 2016 when the IFLA launched the Children Arbitration Scheme.

Family judges have hailed the positive role arbitration can now play as a result of these developments. Baker J noted in 2013 that the resolution of marital disputes by arbitration was 'largely in accordance with the overriding objective of the Family Procedure Rules 2010' and that 'it is always in the interests of parties to try to resolve disputes by agreement wherever possible, including disputes concerning the future of children and ancillary relief of the breakdown of a marriage'.[20] He also highlighted the attractions of arbitration for divorced

---

17 'Arbitration in the Family Court': Practice Guidance issued on 23 November 2015 by Sir James Munby, President of the Family Division, https://www.judiciary.uk/publications/practice-guidance-arbitration-in-the-family-court/ (accessed 21 March 2020).

18 'Arbitration in the Family Court', [12], quoting *S v S* [2014] EWHC 7 (Fam).

19 'Arbitration in the Family Court', [2].

20 *AI v MT* [2013] EWHC 100, at [37], [30].

couples, which include 'speed, confidentiality and cost ... the parties are able to select the arbitrator as opposed to litigation where the parties are obliged to accept the judge allocated to hear the case'.[21]

The seminal precedent laid down in *AI v MT*

AI v MT[22] was a very significant case relating to the role of religious tribunals under arbitration law. The Jewish couple involved in the case asked Baker J during proceedings if they could have their marital dispute arbitrated by a Jewish Beth Din tribunal and agree to be bound by any arbitration award made by the Beth Din. Baker J declined on the basis that making such an order 'flouted the principle that the court's jurisdiction to determine issues arising out of the marriage, or concerning the welfare and upbringing of the children, cannot be ousted by agreement'.[23] He did, however, endorse the couple's decision to refer the dispute to a Beth Din on the basis that the outcome would not be binding unless it received a consent order from the court. The couple's dispute was then successfully resolved by the Beth Din and subsequently affirmed by Baker J via a consent order. Baker J highlighted the success of the case in satisfying both the religious beliefs of the couple as well as the principles of English law, stating:

> This case illustrates the principle propounded by Archbishop Rowan Williams in his 2008 lecture 'Civil and Religious Law in England: a Religious Perspective'... that 'citizenship in a secular society should not necessitate the abandoning of religious discipline, any more than religious discipline should deprive one of access to

21 *AI v MT*, at [32].

22 [2013] EWHC 100 (Fam).

23 *AI v MT*, at [12].

liberties secured by the law of the land, to the common benefits of secular citizenship'.[24]

The case was significant in establishing the first ever precedent of an English court referring a divorce dispute for arbitration to a religious tribunal, with the option of granting the decision legal status via a consent order.[25] The case affirms at the same time that the civil courts retain ultimate jurisdiction over certain post-divorce settlements. A Sharia tribunal or Beth Din may make decisions between parties, but such decisions will not have any legal force. The decision can only be made legally binding by a civil court granting a consent order, which itself will only occur if the court is satisfied that the agreement does not contravene English law.[26]

The Muslim Arbitration Tribunal

Although the Arbitration Act 1996 was chiefly aimed at commercial disputes, its function was by no means limited to litigants in the field of commerce. Due to its broad remit, the Act effectively allowed any group of citizens to refer their civil disputes to private arbitrators rather than refer them to the courts. Section 46 was particularly revolutionary in allowing such citizens to choose a law *other than English law* to be applied by their chosen arbitrator to resolve the dispute. It is this section which gave religious communities such as the Jewish and Muslim communities access to religious-based arbitration, a fact which is vividly illustrated by the formation of the Muslim Arbitration Tribunal (MAT), to which we can now turn.

---

24 *AI v MT*, at [35].

25 See *AI v MT*, at [31], in which Baker J affirms that there is no precedent before the date of his order for referring a matrimonial dispute to arbitration.

26 *AI v MT*, at [33].

When the first major wave of Muslim migration to Britain occurred after the Second World War, large numbers of Muslim migrants who settled in Britain in the 1950s and 1960s established informal mechanisms to resolve religious disputes within their community (Ansari, 2004). Disputants would, for example, organize a meeting with a recognized religious scholar in a mosque, office or even a family home. Such meetings usually lacked any form of specified legal procedure and were informal. The High Court case of *Choudhury v Choudhury*[27] evidences just how informal such occasions were. As Kitchin J notes, the decision was made by the scholar in a meeting arranged 'at the family home' of the disputants.[28]

Faizul Aqtab Siddique was one of the religious scholars who used to resolve disputes for the Muslim community during this period (Bowen, 2013). He was aware that the work he and his fellow Muslim scholars were engaging in was problematic because it was unregulated. This had several negative consequences and meant that decisions made by religious scholars 'often raised more questions than answers'.[29] If, for example, a disputant was not happy with a decision, they could just forum shop and go to another Muslim scholar to seek a more favourable decision.[30] One party could also be unfairly treated by the other party or by the Muslim scholar resolving the dispute because of their gender, for example, or because of their social background.

Based upon the problematic nature of this work, Siddique set up the MAT in 2007, the first of its kind in Britain. A particular advantage was that he was a practising barrister as well as a

27 [2006] EWHC 1837 (Ch).

28 [2006] EWHC 1837 (Ch), at [7].

29 http://matribunal.com/history.php (accessed 27 November 2018).

30 This problematic phenomenon known as 'forum shopping' is an unavoidable feature of the alternative dispute resolution playing field, in which no single player enjoys an exclusive monopoly over the provision of quasi-judicial services (see Sandberg and Thompson, 2016: 183).

Muslim scholar[31] and therefore aware that the Arbitration Act 1996 provided a legal framework which could be utilized to greatly enhance the work of religious dispute resolution bodies. The MAT states that it was established 'to provide a viable alternative for the Muslim community' by seeking to resolve their disputes in accordance with both English and Islamic law.[32] This could be achieved via arbitration, which would 'have the additional benefit of saving the Muslim community the hassle of resorting to costly and time-consuming litigation in the state courts and tribunals'.[33]

Three unique characteristics were highlighted by the MAT which set it apart from the informal practices which Siddique and other Muslim scholars used to engage in.[34] The first is the tribunal's access to an expert panel of legal professionals who specialize in English law, as well as Islamic scholars well versed in both English and Islamic laws. This enables the tribunal to reconcile the spirit of English law with Islamic legal principles when reaching decisions in any of its cases.[35] The second is the appeal to Muslims in modern Britain as the MAT's panel of caseworkers are all British, ensuring cultural awareness and an intimate understanding and experience of modern British society. The third is the contribution of women, who are fully involved in the functioning of the tribunal. This tries to tackle the issue of potential gender bias and provides a more hospitable environment for female clients.[36]

The Arbitration Act had a transformational impact on Siddique's work (Bowen, 2011: 413). The MAT became the first Muslim dispute resolution forum to develop a formal set

---

31 http://www.hijazcollege.com/the-principle.php (accessed 27 November 2018).

32 http://matribunal.com/history.php (accessed 27 November 2018).

33 http://www.matribunal.com/MAT_Forced_%20Marriage_%20Report (accessed 27 November 2018).

34 http://matribunal.com/why-MAT.php (accessed 27 November 2018).

35 http://matribunal.com/why-MAT.php (accessed 27 November 2018).

36 http://matribunal.com/why-MAT.php (accessed 27 November 2018).

of procedural rules which systemized and organized its work, in much the same way as the English civil procedural rules systemize the work of the English courts.[37] As a result, MAT services became more uniform and professional. By virtue of the Act, the decisions made by the MAT could be enforced in the civil courts. The precedent established in *AI v MT* was significant in this regard, confirming that the MAT could apply to the family court for a consent order to enforce its decision in a marital dispute.

Conclusion

The establishment of the MAT meant that the British Muslim community finally had access to an arbitration service which could deal with their religious needs in a culturally sensitive environment. At the same time, the Arbitration Act also ensured that vulnerable members of the Muslim community would not face unfair treatment within the process as the tribunal was bound by the Act's standards of fairness. This latter characteristic is of seminal socio-legal significance when the broader issue of gender discrimination is taken into consideration. Ever since their initial formation in the 1980s, the main criticism of Sharia tribunals in the UK is their behaviour towards female users of their services. This criticism has been amplified by a body of testimonial evidence, steadily accumulating over the two decades since 2000, that gender discrimination is embedded in the practices and procedures of Sharia tribunals. Bano, one of the first researchers to raise concerns about the treatment of women in Sharia tribunals, focused on the experience of South Asian Muslim women who used the services (Bano, 2004) and discovered that many such users felt that several aspects of the process reinforced gender inequality.

37 http://matribunal.com/rules.php (accessed 27 November 2019).

It should be noted that such testimonials will always remain highly subjective. As Douglas states, 'dissatisfaction with dispute resolution services, of any and all kinds, is as old as dispute resolution itself' (Douglas, 2015: 62). There is no doubt that Sharia tribunals do suffer from a number of flaws and shortcomings. What is required, however, is for these flaws and shortcomings to be placed in perspective, as Douglas suggests. Thus, for example, while many clients have reported negative experiences with Sharia tribunals, an equally large number of clients have reported positive experiences with such tribunals. After analysing the case files of over 250 cases dealt with by the Muslim Law Sharia Council and interviewing several clients involved in these cases, Shah-Kazemi found in 2001 that the Council offered Muslim women a much-needed and empowering service (Shah-Kazemi, 2001).

The new Family Arbitration Scheme now opens up new avenues for religious tribunals such as the MAT. Muslim arbitrators would of course have to undergo the requisite training under the scheme and become members of the Chartered Institute of Arbitrators. They would also be limited to applying English law and would still require a consent order to enforce the final decision. Despite these limitations, the scheme offers Muslim arbitrators a welcome opportunity to use their intimate knowledge of cultural sensitivities within the Muslim community to the advantage of Muslim parties seeking the flexibility and cost-effectiveness of family arbitration to resolve their marital disputes.[38]

[38] Some examples of organizations currently purporting to offer arbitration services to the Muslim community within the context of relationship breakdown include the Islamic Council of Europe and the UK Islamic Council, see https://iceurope.org and http://theislamiccouncil.co.uk/mediation-arbitration/ (both accessed 8 November 2019).

ELEVEN

'Regrettably it is not that Simple': the Case for Minimalistic Marriage Laws

Patrick Nash

Introduction

This chapter makes the case for moving towards a minimalistic law of marriage. It begins by noting the problems caused by the complexity of the current law, notably unregistered Muslim 'non-qualifying ceremonies' of marriages (*nikahs*), which should be a key focus of policy makers. While Sharia Councils are often the focus of media and political attention, they are merely a symptom of the inadequacies of English law and the state's absence from this area of social activity. It then proceeds to discuss the first instance decision in the case of *Akhter v Khan*,[1] which unsettled the law's consistency as regards unrecognized Muslim marriages, arguing that the decision was essentially a kludge which created additional confusion and was a poor substitute for legislative intervention. Taking simplicity as its lodestar, and cross-partisan contempt for bureaucracy as its compass (Ferguson, 2014; Graeber, 2015), this chapter provides

1 [2018] EWFC 54. This decision was reversed on appeal: *Attorney General v Akhter and Khan* [2020] EWCA Civ 122.

a brief introduction to 'nudge theory' to sketch out a short plea for a minimalistic law of marriage. Nudge theory emphasizes the need for simplicity, convenience and affordability when it comes to the design of effective law and policy.

Informed by these objectives, a survey of potential options for reform follows, including: assorted unviable solutions; cohabitation law reform; the introduction of compulsory civil registration under the existing regulatory system; and modernising the formalities which govern the entry into legally recognized relationships. The pros, cons and likely obstacles to each alternative will be assessed and then the case made for marriage formalities reform as being the best way forward. The chapter concludes with a prognosis of the prospects for reform, an acknowledgement of the complex social context of Muslim marriages and a final plea for minimalistic marriage laws.

English law vs unrecognized Muslim marriages

'An ill-assorted collection of poorly-matching parts, forming a distressing whole.' One would be hard-pressed to find a better description of contemporary English marriage law than the *Oxford English Dictionary's* definition of a kludge. The current regulatory system has created a situation both 'morally repugnant and economically nonsensical' (Probert and Saleem, 2018: 25), being especially inhospitable towards Muslims, whose marriages go unrecognized on a massive scale. That an overhaul is overdue is uncontroversial; the real challenge is in making a good selection from a menu of potential reforms.

There are numerous basic requirements for the solemnization of a legally valid Muslim marriage. The mosque must first be certified as a place of public worship and then registered for the solemnization of marriages (Marriage Act 1949, s 41(1)). This being done, the parties must give 28 days' notice at the register office (s 26). A civil registrar or authorized person (usually a religious leader) from the registered mosque must be present at the ceremony (s 27(5); s 44(2)(a)), which must be conducted with open doors and in the presence of two witnesses (s 44(2)). The only constraint on the form of the ceremony itself is that prescribed words are used to the effect that the parties are free and agree to marry each other (s 44(3)). The registrar or authorized person must then register the marriage (s 53).

This basic structure is a remnant from a time before large-scale Muslim immigration and is far removed from the typical nature of traditional Muslim marriage ceremonies. By contrast, as Akhtar explains, 'the Nikah (Muslim marriage ceremony) can occur anywhere, at anytime; with no specific ceremony, usually, although not exclusively, in the presence of witnesses' (Akhtar, 2018a: 428). This disparity between forms has meant that Muslim marriages, which frequently satisfy none of the requisite formalities, have been consistently classified as non-marriages (now termed non-qualifying ceremonies[2] without legal consequence [Vora, this volume]).

It is thought that 60–80 per cent of Muslim marriages are conducted outside of the legal framework (Akhtar, 2015, 2018a: 428). The inconvenience of having to have two ceremonies, misconceptions about the legal validity of the *nikah* and the low numbers of registered mosques are all significant factors contributing to the scale of this growing problem (Akhtar, 2015, 2018a, 2018c; Probert and Saleem, 2018: 7–8). As a result, de facto polygamy (a social fact unrecognized by law and therefore beyond the scope of the offence of bigamy) has proliferated, while Muslim women are left unprotected by state law and resort to fee-charging Sharia Councils for redress upon the breakdown of their *nikahs* (Nash, 2017: 524). There may be around 85 of these bodies operating throughout the country, with the vast majority of their business consisting in unregistered Muslim marriages (Nash, 2017: 524). Although performing an important function for

2 Following *Attorney General v Akhter and Khan* [2020] EWCA Civ 122.

those with no recourse to English law, they have generated widespread and legitimate public concern, to say nothing of sensationalist headlines, on account of their discriminatory practices and patriarchal attitudes (Nash, 2017: 524). Indeed, Sharia Councils have become the focal point of the wider debate over Muslim integration and have featured prominently in government inquiries and policy documents (Casey, 2016; Home Office, 2018). That they are largely a symptom of defective marriage laws is easily overlooked by non-specialists given the notorious and ever-deepening complexity of the law of nullity.

As mentioned earlier, the common law typically treated religious-only marriages as legally inconsequential (see Probert, this volume). With the first instance judgment in *Akhter v Khan*,[3] however, even this point of consistency was unsettled, albeit later rejected by the Court of Appeal. Williams J had brought a *nikah* marriage within the law of nullity (classifying it as void and therefore consequential) by using a human rights-based approach to sidestep the usual problems with a typical Islamic ceremony, focusing instead upon the intentions of the parties and their subsequent behaviour. The decision, as the judge was keen to stress, was not to have general application to all *nikahs* despite the public importance of this issue and was decided on its own peculiar factual matrix (para 5). However laudable the outcome, *Akhter* had the potential to open the floodgates on *nikah* litigation where significant assets are at stake as Muslim women turn to the English courts for rulings on their own relationship histories. As one commentator noted, it was likely to give false confidence to Muslim laywomen and create an 'expensive lottery' in fact-based determinations (Amin, 2018). Further, it destabilized the very concept of non-marriages by taking the position that it would be 'deeply unfair to deny a couple who believed themselves to

[3] [2018] EWFC 54.

be married the same legal remedies as a couple [like the one in *Akhter*] who knew they were not' (Probert, 2018a; Barton and Probert, 2018).

The absence of state intervention has allowed marriages conducted outside of the legal framework to grow into a formidable social problem, which spurred Williams J in the first instance decision in *Akhter v Khan* to opt for a suboptimal quick fix, which was rejected on appeal.

What is to be done?

Expecting too much from the law is an ancient folly. Any set of proposals seeking to change popular traditions and alter the social environment on a large scale is open to the charge of being overly ambitious. Nevertheless, 'nudge theory' – a subdiscipline of behavioural economics – demonstrates that mundane alterations to the social environment can induce striking shifts in behaviour (Adida et al, 2016: 150). Its potential to improve governance is evident from the government's creation of a 'nudge unit' known as the Behavioural Insights Team (Halpern, 2016). Wearing a seatbelt, for example, was once seen both as inconvenient and insulting to the driver; usage was low and road traffic mortality rates high. Following mandatory installation of belts in vehicles along with irritating dashboard noises, public awareness campaigns and the threat of penalties, usage has increased drastically over several decades, saving many lives (HMG, 2013; Levitt and Dubner, 2015: 146–50). There is every reason to think that well-designed marriage regulations could meet with similar success, making non-qualifying ceremonies a rarity rather than the norm among Muslim communities. A general marriage law system that maps closely to Muslim practices will stand the best chance of encouraging engagement with the state as well as assuaging concerns about Islam's compatibility with domestic law. This was recognized by the Law Commission in its *Scoping Paper*, which recommended that 'certainty and simplicity' as well as 'respect for individual choice' inform strategy (Law Commission, 2015: 69–70). How, then, to achieve this in practice?

To begin, it is clear what would not work. Crude attempts to ban Sharia Councils ignore the underlying issue and would simply force these bodies – which do serve a purpose in the vacuum left by an absent state – underground (Akhtar, 2015; Home Office, 2018: 23). The more visible they are and the more that is known about them the better until non-legally binding marriages are brought under control via new legislation. Similarly, a blanket recognition of 'the *nikah* itself, regardless of any registration' (Shah, 2013: 148) would be politically unthinkable and ignores the multifarious purposes of the *nikah* for different couples (Akhtar, 2015, 2018a, 2018b, 2018c). Establishing a regulatory body to oversee Sharia Council activities as the *Siddiqui Review* proposed, even had it not been rejected outright by the Home Office,[4] would have introduced additional layers of bureaucracy and, one suspects, committee politicking around the composition of the oversight body (Home Office, 2018: 20).

A more serious proposal is to tackle non-legally binding marriages after the fact by reforming cohabitation law so that *nikahs* become legally consequential. A concise statement of this approach has been given by Vishal Vora, who wishes to see a more formalized hierarchy of marriage validity (Vora, this volume). Attempts at cohabitation law reform typically include a requirement that the couple have lived together for a certain period of time before they can acquire legal recognition of their relationship and hence more robust protections should it break down (Gilmore and Glennon, 2016: 56–7; Fairburn, 2017: 3). Vora's tiered model of cohabitation classification accounts

---

4 Home Office, 'Response to Siddiqui Review', 2 March 2018, https://homeofficemedia.blog.gov.uk/2018/02/02/home-office-in-the-media-02-february-2018/ (accessed 20 November 2019).

for non-legally binding marriages by discarding this typical duration requirement if the couple underwent a religiously recognized ceremony (Vora, 2016c: 98). There are, however, several major defects with this. First, cohabitation reform is likely to be as politically unpalatable to the government as it has always been; it would be unwise to tie the fate of the unrecognized marriage problem to a solution with a proven track record of failure in Parliament. Second, accurate record keeping for legal purposes would be difficult as the state would only receive retrospective notice of the relationship after it had broken down. Third, this effectively creates a discriminatory tiered marriage system which enshrines the second-class status of Muslim relationships in law. It seems dishonest and disrespectful to treat *nikah* marriages as 'cohabitation in another form' when they are closer, both in nature and in terms of how many Muslim couples understand them, to 'marriage in another form' (Akhtar, 2018a: 441–3).

Legal intervention at the beginning of a formal relationship is the only sure way of protecting the state's legitimate interests in the institution of marriage and avoiding some of the pitfalls inherent in the preceding suggestions. Broadly speaking there are two forms this regulation could take.

One option, put forward by *The independent review into the application of sharia law in England and Wales*, would be to introduce compulsory civil registration of religious marriages under threat of criminal sanction. There would be a legal requirement for Muslim couples to civilly register their marriage separately and prior to their religious ceremony while the celebrant would face penalties for failing to ensure that registration took place (Home Office, 2018: 5). This would be unlikely to work in practice, however, as compulsory civil registration of a separate ceremony would be neither convenient nor attractive to Muslim couples, who are understandably more concerned with the religious dimension of the marriage ceremony. There is evidence to suggest that separate or purely civil ceremonies are actually off-putting to

Muslims and there is little demand for them even in mosques which are registered (Probert and Saleem, 2018: 8). The Law Commission correctly noted that this approach would add 'a needless additional hurdle to getting married' along with the attendant costs of having to have both a religious and civil ceremony (Law Commission, 2015: 73–4). What is more, the notion of imposing criminal penalties on celebrants for not complying with civil registration raises legitimate concerns. Shaheen Ali objects that the *Independent review*'s proposals to revamp the relevant but ineffectual offences[5] are tainted by association with the government's counter-extremism agenda, which has 'blurred boundaries between family law and extremism' (Ali, 2018). Rebecca Probert, on the other hand, cautions that revised offences risk becoming a blunt instrument if they are not scrupulously crafted and do not form part of a reform package which makes legally binding marriages easier to achieve for all (Probert, 2018b). In short, the *Review*'s approach does little to make the law more convenient and seems unlikely to attract the 'buy-in' from Muslim couples needed to make it a success.

The more attractive alternative is to legislate 'for greater choice within a simpler legal structure' (Law Commission, 2015: 75) by replacing the existing regulations with a celebrant-based model underpinned by tightly defined criminal offences. A possible model for this is the Labour government's 2002 White Paper *Civil Registration: Vital Change*, which recommended a system whereby celebrants are made responsible for solemnization, civil or religious. Basic national standards would establish the necessary legal formalities and content of ceremonies, while the couple would determine the time and place with the celebrant. Celebrants would have to notify the Registrar General

5 *R v Bham* [1965] 3 All ER 124; *R v Else* [1964] 2 QB 344.

after their appointment by the particular religious group. The government recognized that this 'is more flexible and responsive to the couples' needs and circumstances … [and] brings considerable administrative simplicity in line with the Government's commitment to deregulation and modernisation, but provides appropriate safeguards for this important change in individuals legal status' (Law Commission, 2015: 21). It is worth noting that in Scotland, which operates an organization-and-celebrant-based system (Marriage (Scotland) Act 1977), there are no known issues of unregistered Muslim marriages and reportedly no Sharia Councils either (Home Office, 2018: 4; Vora, 2016b: 140–1). What is more, Scottish mosques seem to have a more symbiotic relationship with Scots law than is the case in England (Wali, 2016).

In order to give real force to this reformed regulatory infrastructure it must be underwritten with potent criminal offences. Needless to say, these must be well designed and limited to dealing with specific problems. For example, de facto polygamy would be relatively straightforward to address by adopting the definition of marriage – 'religious or civil ceremony of marriage (whether or not legally binding)' – already used in relation to forced marriages (Antisocial Behaviour, Crime and Policing Act 2014, s 121(4)). Likewise, an offence to target celebrants who deceive or pressure a party into a religious-only marriage would be another sensible addition to the law's arsenal (Law Commission, 2015: 90; Probert and Saleem, 2018: 24). A general offence of knowingly and wilfully solemnizing a non-legal marriage is also likely to be an important part of the regulatory infrastructure. To avoid being draconian it would need to be carefully qualified. Rather than a blanket clampdown on any and all unrecognized marriages, which would be as clumsy as it was unenforceable, the offence would need to target 'questionable ceremonies' which have the hallmarks of a public marriage on a case-by-case basis.[6] This would place, for example, clandestine dorm room ceremonies between students desiring 'halal' physical relationships without parental consent beyond its scope. These offences, particularly the latter, would not suffice as stand-alone enactments and would not be fit for purpose outside the general reforms to marriage law outlined earlier (Ali, 2018; Probert and Saleem, 2018: 24–5). Given that convenience is to be the key goal of the new law, the hope is that they would not see much action should the revised system work as anticipated.

Although Probert has shown that it would be possible to tinker with the existing system in order to achieve greater coherence (Probert, 2018c), she is nonetheless clear that 'a complete overhaul of marriage law is essential' (Probert, 2018a). The response to the Law Commission's *Scoping Paper* was that 'now is not the right time to develop options for reform to marriage law'.[7] Not long after, however, the *Integrated Communities Strategy Green Paper* indicated that the government was supportive in principle of 'limited reform' via a 'requirement that civil marriages are conducted before or at the same time as religious ceremonies' (MHCLG, 2018: 58). The government then announced in its October 2018 budget that it had asked the Law Commission to propose options for cutting 'unnecessary red tape' so as to reduce costs and ensure greater choice for couples in relation to wedding venue.[8] Fortunately, however, the final terms of reference for the Law Commission were announced in July 2019 and have been set very broadly, covering red-tape reduction, wedding location and registration (Law Commission, 2019).

6 *Hudson v Leigh* [2009] EWHC 1306 (Fam), at [78].

7 Dominic Raab MP, Letter to Law Commission from Justice Minister, September 2017.

8 HM Treasury, Budget 2018 (HC 1629), October 2018, 80, para 5.52.

Conclusion

Williams J's lament in *Akhter* – 'Regrettably it is not that simple'[9] – could apply to the social context in which the law operates as much as to the law itself. Akhtar makes the important point that no solution is capable of accommodating every interpretation of what a *nikah* is or should be (Akhtar, 2015, 2018a). Muslims enter religious-only marriages for all kinds of reasons and the women in them should not be stereotyped as victims (Akhtar, 2015, 2018a). In many cases, particularly among young Muslims, *nikahs* are 'less "creeping Sharia" and more, how can we be boyfriend-girlfriend like everyone else, without "compromising" our beliefs' (Francois-Cerrah, 2015; Akhtar, 2018a: 448). Such intimate relationships can even be taken as a sign of cultural hybridization representative of ongoing integration into western life (Akhtar, 2018a: 427). The upshot of all this is that moral crusading and half-baked reforms may well do more harm than good.

Yet challenging social complexity is a poor excuse for doing nothing. A new formalities system needs to be conscientiously designed and scrupulously drafted but must, as a matter of urgency, establish objective and generally applicable standards. A celebrant-based system with the bare minimum of formalities and clearly defined offences for non-compliance is undoubtedly the best way to achieve this. It would certainly not please everyone, and is likely to have some teething problems as regards scope and application to unconventional forms of marriage, but the open-ended pragmatism of the common law is more than capable of ironing out difficulties on a case-by-case basis.

What is more, revamped marriage regulations could become a cost-effective and low-maintenance way in which the government can kill several birds with one stone. Muslim

---

9 [2018] EWFC 54, at [5].

citizens in general are unnecessarily inconvenienced by the current law, which also leaves the vulnerable party, often the woman, at a severe disadvantage in the event of relationship breakdown. There is no good reason for this to continue. At the same time, the public needs to be reassured that marriage law reform is not about making space for regressive religious practices within the common law. Sharia Councils have become an extremely toxic flashpoint for the media and public; their perceived unaccountability and discriminatory practices are not an imaginary problem and the *Siddiqui Review* was right to push for a reduction in their de facto power over non-qualifying ceremonies. In the end, British Muslims are far more likely to make use of English law if it is straightforward, inexpensive and convenient. Nudges, not kludges, are the policy maker's best hope.

TWELVE

Conclusion

Rajnaara C. Akhtar, Patrick Nash and Rebecca Probert

As Gillian Douglas has pointed out, all societies have rules governing entry into and exit from marriage 'and the question of who has the power to set and apply these rules has always been the subject of dispute', since it 'enables control to be exerted over the imposition and enforcement of obligations between individuals' (Douglas, 2015: 53). That power may lie with the state, or with religious groups, or indeed individuals. The rules that are laid down may require compliance with specific formal requirements or rituals, or may accord the status of 'marriage' to those who have demonstrated an intention to be married, or lived their lives in a certain way. If we review practices across the globe, we can find examples of all of these different ways of regulating marriage.

So it is worth bearing in mind, as we contemplate how the law might regulate marriage in the future, that there is nothing inevitable about either the current law or indeed religious rituals. Wendy Leeds-Hurwitz quite rightly points out that '[r]ituals have meaning for us because we conveniently forget that we ourselves have designed them' (Leeds-Hurwitz, 2002: 29) and the same point can be made, with equal force, about the legal requirements.

The history of marriage law in England and Wales is one of religious regulation gradually being replaced by legal regulation. Weddings in the Anglican church may involve no direct contact with the state by the couple themselves – they are not obliged to go to the register office to give notice, for example – but it still takes place within a legal framework. Jewish and Quaker weddings, while more lightly regulated than those of other religious groups, must be still preceded by notice. At the same time, the law does accommodate religious diversity. Legally binding marriages can take place according to such rites as the couple may choose as long as they are conducted in a place of worship that has been registered for the purpose. As Stephen Cretney has pointed out, the 1836 legislation was based on the simple principle that the state

> had a proper interest in defining the basic principles of what constituted a marriage … and it was for the State to establish a procedure whereby it could be determined whether or not a person was married … But so far as the actual celebration of the marriage was concerned, the State's role was limited to ensuring that the ceremony be recognised by both parties as binding. (Cretney, 2007: 162)

That the legislation has lasted so long can be seen as a sign of its flexibility: by not listing all of the religious groups that could solemnize marriages but simply allowing any religious group with a building and a sufficient number of adherents to do so, the legal framework could accommodate new religious groups.

That is not to say that the current law is satisfactory. Far from it. There is broad agreement that the current law of marriage is unsatisfactory and outdated and should be reformed. As the chapters in this volume demonstrate, there is less consensus as to how that should be achieved. One option – not advocated by any of the contributors to this volume but with a number of adherents – is to introduce universal civil marriage. The argument is that couples would then be free to have such ceremony as they chose and that the state would not need to engage with the practices of different religious and belief groups. Yet it is difficult to see why those couples who do not take advantage of the option to have a legally recognized marriage in a mosque (by giving notice and undertaking their ceremony in a mosque that has been registered for marriage, in the presence of an authorized person) would be any more willing to enter into a civil marriage. We know from the experience of other jurisdictions that requiring couples to engage in a civil ceremony as a condition of legal recognition – and even explicit provisions criminalizing religious ceremonies that pre-date the civil ceremony – do not prevent religious-only marriages from taking place (Moors et al, 2018).

The Law Commission has made clear that it is not looking to introduce universal civil marriage, but rather to devise a system that would give couples greater choice within a simpler legal structure. Yet any system of formalities will, inevitably, mean that some ceremonies will not comply. It has been suggested by a number of contributors that the law should recognize all religious ceremonies of marriage. Yet even this does not necessarily ensure legal recognition of every ceremony that takes place. Who, after all, decides on what counts as a ceremony of marriage within a particular religious tradition? Depending on its requirements, a couple may regard themselves as married but find that their religion does not share their view. We might take the example of Jewish marriages, which were exempted from the requirements of the Clandestine Marriages Act 1753. Their validity depended on Jewish law – but in a number of cases that came before the courts the advice of the Jewish authorities was that the marriage would not be recognized under Jewish law. In *Goldsmid v Bromer*,[1] for example, the ceremony had been performed but the view was that it had not been attested by competent witnesses. In the eyes of Jewish law – and therefore of English law at that time – it was not legally recognized. No one with any knowledge of

1 (1798) 161 ER 568.

religious courts – for example the church courts that regulated marriage in England and Wales before 1857 – could assume that decisions as to what constitutes a marriage are simple ones. Even if the majority of religious marriages were to be afforded legal recognition, there would be always be some that were not.

History, as well as modern empirical research, also teaches us that views may diverge between the parties as to the nature of the ceremony that they have gone through. One – perhaps overlooked – advantage of having a legal process for getting married is that it provides certainty about the intentions of both parties. It is striking that in a number of cases that have come before the courts, the intentions of the parties seem to have diverged. In both *Hudson v Leigh* and *Akhter v Khan*, there had been a plan – or at least an assumption – that a legally binding civil ceremony would follow the religious one. The same could be said of a number of cases involving cohabitants where one partner expected that the relationship would move towards marriage and the other was less keen.

So decisions will always need to be made as to what rights should be afforded to couples living outside a legally recognized relationship. Here the parallels between those who are cohabiting without any ceremony and those who have gone through a ceremony that has not been afforded legal recognition need to be considered. Some cohabitants would like legal recognition, others are cohabiting precisely to avoid legal rights and responsibilities. Similarly, some couples in religious-only marriages want their marriage to be recognized by the law as such, while others have deliberately chosen the option of non-recognition. As a number of contributors have emphasized, these parallels cannot be overlooked and it would be wrong to regulate one group without considering the implications for the other. Much would depend on the rationale for regulation. If the focus is on the vulnerability of those individuals left without legal redress at the end of a relationship, then it makes little sense to devise remedies that address one but not the other, unless there is evidence that going through a religious-only ceremony – or, less plausibly, living together without any ceremony – makes certain individuals uniquely vulnerable. In the light of the evidence as to the continuing hold of the common-law marriage myth, it cannot be assumed that those who are cohabiting have made an informed choice to opt out of legal rights and responsibilities.

The idea that couples should have the right to opt out if they so choose is one that resonates for a number of contributors. Again, the parallels between those who are cohabiting without any ceremony and those who have gone through a ceremony that has not been afforded legal recognition need to be recognized. When the Law Commission proposed a scheme for conferring rights on cohabiting couples, it made provision for couples to opt out by agreement, so that those who had made a conscious choice to avoid legal rights could ensure that this choice was respected. Those who have gone through a ceremony of marriage already have the option of divesting themselves of many of the obligations of marriage by means of a pre- or post-nuptial agreement, but should they also be able to divest themselves of the very status of marriage by agreement?

As this volume goes to print, marriage law in England and Wales is on the cusp of change. As a number of contributors to this volume have noted, such change may come from different directions. At the time of writing, the Court of Appeal had just published its decision in the appeal of the judgement in *Akhter v Khan*, and it wholly rejected the creative and flexible approach taken by Williams J at first instance.[2] There are indications that the introduction of a schedule system will be initiated by regulations under the Civil Partnership, Marriages and Deaths (Registration etc) Act 2019, although this seems to have been less of a priority than the introduction of civil partnerships for opposite-sex couples. The prospect of a move

2 *Attorney General v Akhter and Khan* [2020] EWCA Civ 122.

away from marriage registers raises questions as to whether the law still needs to regulate who is responsible for registering a marriage to the same extent (Probert, 2017). And alongside the Law Commission's wide-ranging review of marriage law, the government is still exploring the option of 'limited reform relating to the law on marriage and religious weddings, based on the recommendations of the Independent Sharia Review'.[3]

Some of these reforms may be more welcome than others. Yet we feel that there is room for optimism. As John Eekelaar has pointed out in recommending reform:

> our marriage law, confused though it is, has developed by making a series of accommodations with various groups and points of view … . Most people see marriage as a major event in their personal lives, which for many can only be adequately expressed if it has been brought about in a manner in accordance with a deeply held belief, or in a way that holds strong meaning for them.

The law has accommodated different groups in the past, and the Law Commission has expressly identified the aim of its project as being to devise a system that will give couples greater choice within a simpler legal structure. Our hope is that the evidence presented in the preceding chapters will assist policy makers in understanding the complexities of regulating marriage (and cohabitation) and will put the legal formalities in a wider context, and that reforms result in a marriage law that is fit for our diverse 21st-century society.

---

3 https://www.lawcom.gov.uk/project/weddings/ (accessed 21 March 2020).

References

Adida, C., Laitin, D. and Valfort, M.A. (2016) *Why Muslim Integration Fails in Christian-Heritage Societies*, Cambridge MA: Harvard University Press.

Ahmed, F. and Norton, J.C. (2012) 'Religious Tribunals, Religious Freedom, and Concern for Vulnerable Women', *Child and Family Law Quarterly*, 24(4): 363–88.

Akhtar, R.C. (2013) 'Towards Conceptualising User-Friendly Shari'a Councils', *Journal of Islamic State Practices in International Law*, 9(2): 112–35.

Akhtar, R.C. (2015) 'Unregistered Muslim Marriages: An Emerging Culture of Celebrating Rites and Compromising Rights' in J. Miles, P. Mody and R. Probert (eds), *Marriage Rites and Rights*, Oxford: Hart, pp 167–92.

Akhtar, R.C. (2018a) 'Modern Traditions in Muslim Marriage Practices, Exploring English Narratives', *Oxford Journal of Law and Religion*, 7(3): 427–54.

Akhtar, R. (2018b) 'The Human Right to Marry: A Refugee's Perspective', *Journal of Social Welfare and Family Law*, 40(2): 262–9.

Akhtar, R.C. (2018c) 'Unregistered Muslim Marriages in the UK; Examining Normative Influences Shaping Choice of Legal Protection' in M.C. Foblets, M. Graziadei and A.D. Runteln (eds), *Personal Autonomy in Plural Societies, A Principle and Its Paradoxes*, Abingdon: Routledge, pp 140–55.

Akhtar, R.C. (2019) 'Plural Approaches to Faith-Based Dispute Resolution by Britain's Muslim Communities', *Child and Family Law Quarterly*, 31(3): 189–210.

Albakri, M., Hill, S., Kelley, N. and Rahim, N. (2019) 'Relationships and Gender Identity' in J. Curtice, E. Clery, J. Perry, M. Phillips and N. Rahim (eds), *British Social Attitudes: The 36th Report*, London: NatCen, pp 1–28.

Ali, K. (2008) 'Marriage in Classical Islamic Jurisprudence: A Survey of Doctrines' in A. Quraishi and F.E. Vogel (eds), *The Islamic Marriage Contract*, Cambridge MA: Harvard University Press, pp 11–45.

Ali, S. (2018) Symposium on *The independent review into the application of Sharia law in England and Wales* by the UK Home Office, Sharia Source at Harvard Law School, 19 March 2018, https://shariasource.blog/2018/03/19/symposium-on-the-independent-review-into-the-application-of-sharia-law-in-england-and-wales-by-the-uk-home-office/

Amin, M. (2018) 'Has English law recognised a "nikah only" marriage?' https://www.mohammedamin.com/Community_issues/Nikah-only-marriage-recognised.html

An-Naim, A.A. (ed) (2002) *Islamic Family Law in a Changing World: A Global Resource Book*, London: Zed Books.

An-Naim, A.A. (2010) 'Compatibility Dialectic: Mediating the Legitimate Coexistence of Islamic Law and State Law', *Modern Law Review*, 73(1): 1–29.

Ansari, H. (2004) *The Infidel Within: Muslims in Britain since 1800*, London: Hurst & Company.

Arshad, R. (2010) *Islamic Family Law*, London: Sweet & Maxwell.

Bano, S. (2004) 'Complexity, Difference and "Muslim Personal Law": Rethinking the Relationship between Shariah Councils and South Asian Muslim Women in Britain' (University of Warwick, PhD thesis).

Bano, S. (2007) Islamic Family Arbitration, Justice and Human Rights in Britain, *Law, Social Justice & Global Development Journal*, 1: 1–27.

Bano, S. (2008) 'In Pursuit of Religious and Legal Diversity: A Response to the Archbishop of Canterbury and the "Shari'a Debate" in Britain', *Ecclesiastical Law Journal* 10(3): 283–309.

Bano, S. (2012) *Muslim Women and Shari'ah Councils: Transcending the Boundaries of Community and Law*, Basingstoke: Palgrave Macmillan.

Bano, S. (2013) 'Muslim Dispute Resolution in Britain: Towards a New Framework of Family Law Governance?' in M. Maclean and J. Eekelaar (eds), *Managing Family Justice in Diverse Societies*, Oxford: Hart, pp 61–86.

Barlow, A. and James, G. (2004) 'Regulating Marriage and Cohabitation in 21st Century Britain', *Modern Law Review* 67(2): 143–76.

Barlow, A. and Smithson, J. (2010) 'Legal Assumptions, Cohabitants' Talk and the Rocky Road to Reform', *Child and Family Law Quarterly*, 22(3): 328–50.

Barlow, A., Duncan, S., James, G. and Park, A. (2001), 'Just a Piece of Paper? Marriage and Cohabitation in Britain' in A. Park, J. Curtice, K. Thomson, L. Jarvis and C. Bromley (eds), *British Social Attitudes: The 18th Report*, London: Sage, pp 31–57.

Barlow, A., Duncan, S., James, G. and Park, A. (2005) *Cohabitation, Marriage and the Law – Social Change and Legal Reform in the 21st Century*, Oxford: Hart.

Barlow, A., Burgoyne C. and Smithson, J. (2007) 'The Living Together Campaign', *Family Law* (February): 165–8.

Barlow, A., Burgoyne C., Clery, E. and Smithson, J. (2008) 'Cohabitation and the Law: Myths, Money and the Media' in A. Park, J. Curtis and K. Thompson (eds), *British Social Attitudes: The 24th Report*, London: Sage, pp 29–52.

Barton, C. and Probert, R. (2018) 'The Status of a Religious-only Marriage: Valid, Void or "Non"? *Akhter v Khan*', *Family Law* 48: 1540–7.

Black, A., Esmaeili, H. and Hosen, N. (2013) *Modern Perspectives on Islamic Law*, Cheltenham: Edward Elgar Publishing.

Blacklett, R. (2009) 'The Status of Religious "Courts" in English Law', *Disputes and International Arbitration Newsletter*, 11.

Bonthuys, E. (2016) 'A Patchwork of Marriages: The Legal Relevance of Marriage in a Plural Legal System', *Onati Socio-Legal Series* [online] 6(6).

Bowen, J. (2011) 'How Could English Courts Recognise Shariah?', *University of St. Thomas Law Journal* 7(3): 411–35.

Bowen, J. (2013) 'Sanctity and Shariah: Two Islamic Modes of Resolving Disputes in Todays England' in F. von Benda-Beckmann (ed), *Religion in Disputes: Pervasiveness of Religious Normativity in Disputing Process*, New York: Palgrave Macmillan, pp 129–45.

Bowen, J.R. (2016) *On British Islam: Religion, Law, and Everyday Practice in Shari'a Councils.* Oxford: Princeton University Press.

Casey, L. (2016) The Casey Review: A Review into Opportunity and Integration, London: Department for Communities and Local Government.

Centre for Social Cohesion (2009) *The Beth Din: Jewish Courts in the UK*, London: Centre for Social Cohesion.

Chukwumerije, O. (1999) 'Judicial Supervision of Commercial Arbitration: The English Arbitration Act 1996', *Arbitration International* 15(2): 171–91.

Cranmer, F. and Thompson, S. (2018) 'Marriage and Civil Partnership in Northern Ireland: A Changing Legal Landscape', *Child and Family Law Quarterly* 30(3): 301–20.

Cretney, S. (2007) 'Relationships: Law Content and Form' in J. Trowell and C. Thorpe (eds), *Re-Rooted Lives, Inter-disciplinary Work within the Family Justice System* (2nd edn), Bristol: Jordans, 4(2).

Diduck, A. (2016) 'Autonomy and Family Justice', *Child and Family Law Quarterly* 28(2): 133–49.

Douglas, G. (2015) 'Who Regulates Marriage? The Case of Religious Marriage and Divorce' in R. Sandberg (ed), *Religion and Legal Pluralism*, Farnham, Ashgate, pp 53–66.

Douglas, G., Doe, N., Gilliat-Ray, S., Sandberg, R. and Khan, A. (2011) *Social Cohesion and Religious Law: Marriage, Divorce and Religious Courts*, Cardiff: Cardiff Law School.

Douglas, G., Doe, N., Gilliat-Ray, S., Sandberg, R. and Khan, A. (2012) 'The Role of Religious Tribunals in Regulating Marriage and Divorce', *Child and Family Law Quarterly* 24(2): 139–57.

Duncan, S. (2011) 'Personal Life, Pragmatism and Bricoloage', *Sociological Research Online* 16(4).

Duncan, S., Barlow, A. and James, G. (2005) 'Why Don't They Marry? Cohabitation, Commitment and DIY Marriage', *Child and Family Law Quarterly* 17(3): 383–98.

Edge, I. (2013) 'Islamic Finance, Alternative Dispute Resolution and Family Law: Developments Towards Legal Pluralism?' in R. Griffith Jones (ed), *Islam and English Law*, Cambridge: Cambridge University Press, pp 116–43.

Eekelaar, J. (2013) 'Marriage: A Modest Proposal', *Family Law* 43(1): 83–5.

Esposito, J.L. and DeLong-Bas, N.J. (2001) *Women in Muslim Family Law* (2nd edn), New York: Syracuse University Press.

Fairburn, C. (2017) '"Common Law Marriage" and Cohabitation', HoC Briefing Paper No 03372, London: House of Commons Library.

Fairbairn, C., Kennedy S., McGuinness, T. and Thurley, D. (2017) 'Polygamy', HoC Briefing Paper No 05051, London: House of Commons Library.

Fawcett Society (2010) *Keeping Mum*, London: Fawcett Society.

Ferguson, L. (2013) 'Arbitration in Financial Dispute Resolution: The Final Step to Reconstructing the Default(s) and Exception(s)?', *Journal of Social Welfare and Family Law* 35(1): 115–38.

Ferguson, N. (2014) *The Great Degeneration*, London: Penguin.

Francois-Cerrah, M. (2015) 'Sharia Marriage in the UK Is Not Toxic – Polygamous Men Are', *The Telegraph*, 3 July.

Gaffney-Rhys, R. (2010) '*Hudson v Leigh* – the Concept of the Non-marriage', *Child and Family Law Quarterly* 22(3): 351–65.

Gilmore, S. and Glennon, L. (2016) *Hayes and Williams' Family Law* (5th edn), Oxford: Oxford University Press.

Gohir, S. (2015) 'Media Scares about "Sharia Marriages" Miss the Point', *The Guardian*, 6 July.

Graeber, D. (2015) *The Utopia of Rules*, London: Melville House.

Halpern, D. (2016) *The Nudge Unit*, London: WH Allen.

Hanna, S. and Lowes, E. (2018) 'The Problem with Nikah Contracts and Other Marriages', *Private Client Business* 4: 133.

HMG (2013) 'Thirty Years of Seatbelt Safety', https://www.gov.uk/government/news/thirty-years-of-seatbelt-safety

Home Office (2018) *The independent review into the application of sharia law in England and Wales*, CM 9560.

Hunter, M. (1987) 'Judicial Assistance for the Arbitrator' in J. Lew (ed), *Contemporary Problems in International Arbitration*, London: Springer, pp 195–206.

Islamic Sharia Council (nd) http://www.islamic-sharia.org/aboutus/

Jaan, H. (2014) *Equal and Free? 50 Muslim Women's Experiences of Marriage in Britain Today*, Islamabad: Aurat Foundation.

Kennett, W. (2016) 'It's Arbitration, But Not As We Know It: Reflections on Family Law Dispute Resolution', *International Journal of Law, Policy and the Family* 30(1): 1–31.

Knights, S. (2007) *Freedom of Religion, Minorities and the Law*, Oxford: Oxford University Press.

Law Commission (1971) *Family Law: Polygamous Marriages*, Law Com No 42, London: HMSO.

Law Commission (2006) *Cohabitation: The Financial Consequences of Relationship Breakdown*, Law Com CP No 179, London: TSO.

Law Commission (2007) *Cohabitation: The Financial Consequences of Relationship Breakdown*, Law Com No 307, London: TSO.

Law Commission (2011) *Intestacy and Family Provision Claims on Death*, Law Com No 331, London: TSO.

Law Commission (2015) *Getting Married: A Scoping Paper*, London: TSO.

Law Commission (2018) https://www.lawcom.gov.uk/project/weddings/

Law Commission (2019) 'Law Commission begins work on weddings reform', https://www.lawcom.gov.uk/law-commission-begins-work-on-weddings-reform/

Leahy, S. and O'Sullivan, K. (2018) 'Changing Conceptions of Marriage in Ireland: Law and Practice', *Child and Family Law Quarterly* 30(3): 279–300.

Leeds-Hurwitz, W. (2002) *Wedding as Text: Communicating Cultural Identities Through Ritual*, Mahwah: Lawrence Erlbaum Associates.

Le Grice, V. (2013) 'A Critique of Non-marriage', *Family Law*, 43(10): 1278–85.

Levitt, S. and Dubner, S. (2015) *Superfreakonomics*, London: Penguin.

MacEoin, D. (2009) *Sharia Law or 'One Law for All?'*, London: Civitas.

Manea, E. (2016) *Women and Sharia Law: The Impact of Legal Pluralism in the UK*, London: IB Tauris.

McLean, M. (2018) 'Beyond Belief: The Law and Practice of Marriage Formation in Contemporary Scotland', *Child and Family Law Quarterly* 30(3): 237–57.

Mehta, A. (2015) 'Schedule 1 to The Children Act 1989: Not Just for Wags', *Family Law Week*, 6 February.

MHCLG (Ministry of Housing, Communities and Local Government) (2018) *Integrated Communities Strategy Green Paper.*

MHCLG (2019a) *Integrated Communities Strategies: Summary of consultation response and Government response.*

MHCLG (2019b) *Integrated Communities Action Plan.*

Mohee, S. (2011) 'Young British South Asian Muslim Women: Identities and Marriage' (University College London, PhD thesis).

Moors, A., de Koning, M. and Vroon-Najem, V. (2018) 'Secular Rule and Islamic Ethics: Engaging with Muslim-Only Marriages in the Netherlands', *Sociology of Islam* 6(3): 274–96.

Muslim Council of Britain Report (2015) 'British Muslims in Numbers, A Demographic, Socio-economic and Health Profile of Muslims in Britain Drawing on the 2011 Census', https://www.mcb.org.uk/wp-content/uploads/2015/02/MCBCensusReport_2015.pdf

Muslim Marriage Working Group (2012) *Report of Working Group.*

Namazie, M., Atasheen, Y., Waters, A. and Seltman, M. (2010) *Sharia Law in Britain: A Threat to One Law for All & Equal Rights*, London: One Law for All.

Naqvi, Z.B. (2017a) 'A Contextualised Historical Account of Changing Judicial Attitudes to Polygamous Marriage in the English Courts', *International Journal of Law in Context* 13(3): 408–28.

Naqvi, Z.B. (2017b) 'Critical Feminist Perspectives on the Legal Recognition of Polygamous Marriages in the UK' (University of Birmingham, PhD thesis).

Nash, P. (2017) 'Sharia in England: The Marriage Law Solution', *Oxford Journal of Law and Religion* 6(3): 523–43.

ONS (Office of National Statistics) (2014) 'Marriages in England and Wales: 2014'.

ONS (2017a) 'Births by Parents' Characteristics in England and Wales: 2016'.

ONS (2017b) 'Marriages in England and Wales: 2014'.

ONS (2018a) 'Families and the Labour Market, England: 2018'.

ONS (2018b) 'Muslim Population in the UK'.

ONS (2018c) 'Marriages in England and Wales: 2015'.

ONS (2019) 'Families and Households in the UK: 2018'.

O'Sullivan, K. and Jackson L. (2017) 'Muslim Marriage (Non) Recognition: Implications and Possible Solutions', *Journal of Social Welfare and Family* 39(1): 22–41.

Parveen, R. (2017) 'Do Sharia Councils Meet the Needs of Muslim Women?' in S. Bano (ed), *Gender and Justice in Family Law Disputes: Women, Mediation and Religious Arbitration*, Waltham MA: Brandeis University Press, pp 142–65.

Parveen, R. (2018a) 'Do Shari'a Councils Meet the Needs of Muslim Women?' (University of Birmingham, PhD thesis).

Parveen, R. (2018b) 'Religious-Only Marriages in the UK: Legal Positionings and Muslims Women's Experiences', *Sociology of Islam* 6(3): 1–24.

Pearl, D. and Menski, W. (1998) *Muslim Family Law* (3rd edn), London: Sweet & Maxwell.

Probert, R. (2002) 'When are we married? Void, non-existent and presumed marriages', *Legal Studies* 22(3): 398–419.

Probert, R. (2009a) *Marriage Law and Practice in the Long Eighteenth Century: A Reassessment*, Cambridge: Cambridge University Press.

Probert, R. (2009b) 'Cohabitation – Current Legal Solutions', *Current Legal Problems* 62(1): 316–45.

Probert, R. (2012) *The Changing Legal Regulation of Cohabitation: From Fornicators to Family, 1600–2010*, Cambridge: Cambridge University Press.

Probert, R. (2013) 'The Evolving Concept of "Non-marriage"', *Child and Family Law Quarterly* 25(3): 314–35.

Probert, R. (2017) 'The registration of marriage', *Family Law* 1103.

Probert, R. (2018a) 'Roundtable on Islamic Family Law in the UK: Engaging with the Terms of the Marriage Act of 1949', Sharia Source at Harvard Law School, 23 August, https://shariasource.blog/2018/08/23/roundtable-on-islamic-family-law-in-the-uk-engaging-with-the-terms-of-the-marriage-act-of-1949/

Probert, R. (2018b) 'Criminalising Non-compliance with Marriage Formalities?', *Family Law* 48(6): 702–6.

Probert, R. (2018c) 'A Uniform Marriage Law for England and Wales?', *Child and Family Law Quarterly* 30(3): 259–78.

Probert, R. and Saleem, S. (2018) 'The Legal Treatment of Islamic Marriage Ceremonies', *Oxford Journal of Law and Religion* 7(3): 1–25.

Pywell, S. and Probert R. (2018) 'Neither Sacred nor Profane: The Permitted Content of Civil Marriage Ceremonies', *Child and Family Law Quarterly* 30(4): 415–36.

Qureshi, K. (2016) *Marital Breakdown among British Asians: Conjugality, Legal Pluralism and New Kinship*, Basingstoke: Palgrave Macmillan.

Ramadan, T. (2004) *Western Muslims and the Future of Islam*, Oxford: Oxford University Press.

Read, F. (2012) 'Resolution International Committee: Non-recognition of Islamic Marriages in England and Wales', *International Family Law* 11: 452–4.

Redfern, A. (1986) 'International Commercial Arbitration, Jurisdiction Denied: The Pyramid Collapses', *Journal of Business Law* 15: 15–22.

Sandberg, R. and Thompson S. (2016) 'The Sharia Law Debate: The Missing Family Law Context', *Law and Justice* 177: 181–92.

Shachar, A. (2005) 'Religion, State and the Problem of Gender: New Modes of Citizenship and Governance in Diverse Societies', *McGill Law Journal* 50: 49–88.

Shachar, A. (2013) 'Privatising Diversity: A Cautionary Tale from Religious Arbitration in Family Law' in M.A. Fallinger, E.R. Schiltz and S.J. Stable (eds), *Feminism, Law, and Religion*, Farnham: Ashgate, pp 109–40.

Shah, P. (2013) 'Judging Muslims' in R. Griffith-Jones (ed), *Islam and English Law*, Cambridge: Cambridge University Press, pp 144–56.

Shah-Kazemi, S.N. (2001) *Untying the Knot: Muslim Women, Divorce and the Shariah*, London: Nuffield Foundation.

Smart, C. and Stevens, P. (2000) *Cohabitation Breakdown*, London/York: FPSS/JRF.

Sonneveld, N. (2012) 'Rethinking the Difference Between Formal and Informal Marriages in Egypt' in M. Voorhoeve (ed), *Family Law in Islam*, London: IB Tauris, pp 77–109.

Thompson, S. (2015) *Prenuptial Agreements and the Presumption of Free Choice: Issues of Power in Theory and Practice*, Oxford: Hart.

True Vision (2017) 'The Truth about Muslim Marriages', http://truevisiontv.com/films/details/295/the-truth-about-muslim-marriage

Tucker, J.E. (2008) *Women, Family, and Gender in Islamic Law*, Cambridge: Cambridge University Press.

Uddin, I. (2018) 'Nikah-only Marriages: Causes, Motivations and Their Impact on Dispute Resolution and Islamic Divorce Proceedings in England and Wales', *Oxford Journal of Law and Religion*, 7(3): 401–26.

Voorhoeve, M. (2018) 'Law and Social Change in Tunisia: The Case of Unregistered Marriage', *Oxford Journal of Law and Religion*, 7(3): 479–97.

Vora, V. (2016a) 'The Islamic Marriage Conundrum: Register or Recognize? The Legal Consequences of the Nikah in England and Wales' (SOAS, PhD thesis), https://ethos.bl.uk/OrderDetails.do?uin=uk.bl.ethos.739383

Vora, V. (2016b) 'Unregistered Muslim Marriages in England and Wales: The Issue of Discrimination through "Non-Marriage" Declaration' in Y. Suleiman and P. Anderson (eds), *Muslims in the UK and Europe II*, Cambridge: Cambridge University Press, pp 140–1.

Vora, V. (2016c) 'The Problem of Unregistered Muslim Marriage: Questions and Solutions', *Family Law* 40(1): 95–8.

Wali, K. (2016) 'Divorce in Scots Law and Sharia Law', *The Journal of the Law Society of Scotland*, 14 March.

Walker, T. (2016) *Shari'a Councils and Muslim Women in Britain: Rethinking the Role of Power and Authority*, Leiden: BRILL.

Index

Y

Printed and bound by CPI Group (UK) Ltd, Croydon, CR0 4YY

18/09/2026

14965016-0002